Lessons from the Masters: Improving Narrative Writing

Amanda Hartman and Julia Mooney
Lucy Calkins, series editor

Photography by Peter Cunningham

HEINEMANN ◆ PORTSMOUTH, NH

This book is dedicated to Sophie and Zachary; may the books you love inspire the stories you tell.

Heinemann
361 Hanover Street
Portsmouth, NH 03801–3912
www.heinemann.com

Offices and agents throughout the world

The authors and publisher wish to thank those who have generously given permission to reprint borrowed material:

From *Owl Moon* by Jane Yolen, copyright © 1987 by Jane Yolen. Used by permission of Philomel Books, a division of Penguin Group (USA) Inc. and Curtis Brown, Ltd.

From *The Leaving Morning* by Angela Johnson. Text copyright © 1992 by Angela Johnson. Reprinted by permission of Orchard Books, an imprint of Scholastic Inc.

Cataloging-in-Publication data is on file with the Library of Congress.

ISBN-13: 978-0-325-04728-7

Production: Elizabeth Valway, David Stirling, and Abigail Heim
Cover and interior designs: Jenny Jensen Greenleaf
Series includes photographs by Peter Cunningham, Nadine Baldasare, and Elizabeth Dunford
Composition: Publishers' Design and Production Services, Inc.
Manufacturing: Steve Bernier

Printed in the United States of America on acid-free paper
21 20 19 18 17 VP 2 3 4 5 6

Acknowledgments

THIS BOOK may have been authored by the two of us, but it would never have seen the light of day without a ton of support from others along the way. First and foremost, we extend our thanks to Lucy Calkins for giving us the opportunity to write this book together—and for her brilliant direction and incredible talent for taking a book from solid draft to publication. Thanks also for her extensive help as coauthor of the original book, *Authors as Mentors,* that provided the shoulders on which this book stands.

Second, we thank Kate Montgomery for her guiding light throughout this project. It meant so much to have Kate at our side, with her keen insight, endless support, and willingness to roll up her sleeves and dig in when we most needed her. A big thanks to Felicia O'Brian for the ever important work of sharpening and clarifying parts to ensure a coherent whole. To Heather Anderson, we are grateful for the hours spent wading through the many handwritten edits. And last but not least, Abby Heim has been a constant source of organization and support. We are grateful for her intelligence and humor and for her enormous patience throughout this process.

Next, we extend our gratitude to the entire staff of the Reading and Writing project. This book stands on the shoulders of all that this extraordinary community does, day in and day out, as it seeks to outgrow its best thinking. In particular, we thank our leaders, Laurie Pessah, Kathleen Tolan, Mary Ehrenworth, Audra Robb, Cheryl Tyler, and of course, Lucy, and the terrific team of primary staff developers: Shanna, Christine, Natalie, Lauren, Monique, Celena, Rebecca, Lindsay, Rachel, Katie, Sadia, Marjorie, Ellen, Beth, Enid, Sarah, Elizabeth, and Brianna. We would also like to recognize Kalei Sabaratnam for helping us to organize the student work—no small task!

We certainly couldn't have done this work without the collaboration of schools, teachers, and children. In particular, we would like to thank Adele Schroeder and Katherine Nigen at PS 59M and Anthony Inzerillo, Clara Orban, and Brittany Schwartz at PS 199Q for opening their doors and classrooms and letting us see what second-graders can do when there are people who believe in them. Their stories and thinking is woven throughout this book, so that you, too, can see what's possible.

The class described in this unit is a composite class, with children and partnerships of children gleaned from classrooms in very different contexts, then put together here. We wrote the units this way to bring you both a wide array of children and also to illustrate for you the predictable (and unpredictable) situations and responses this unit has created in classrooms across the nation and world.

We spent many an hour, side by side, in Espresso 77 and Communitea, two very special coffee shops in Queens, where we live. It's not easy finding a writing spot that fuels both your body and mind.

Both of us feel strongly that the support of our families and friends kept us going when we most wanted to stop. Thank you for listening and believing.

Much of our inspiration for the teaching in this book came from the mentor texts: *The Leaving Morning* and *Owl Moon.* Angela Johnson and Jane Yolen, thank you for writing such beautiful books, rich in craft and meaning—books that now feel like old friends. It is your words and your stories that especially brought our book to life.

Lastly, we would like to thank each other for the support, willingness to rethink ideas, and above all for the friendship. Throughout this process, we drew on our complementary talents; we couldn't have done it without each other, and the book is better for this combined effort.

May this book lead you and your students on new journeys of thought and writing. Enjoy!

—Amanda and Julia

Contents

Registration instructions to access the digital resources that accompany this book may be found on p. ix.

Welcome to the Unit

SECOND GRADE IS A SPECIAL YEAR in children's writing lives. The kids are growing up, and they are able to write with greater facility and sophistication. And they are eager to be given important new challenges. Launching the year with a unit in which they take lessons from the "masters" is a way of saying to them, "You're grown-up writers now, ready to write like the best of the best."

Your students will respond to your confidence in them. Many of them will come to school with two years of writing workshop under their belts, and they will therefore be especially ready to carry on with greater independence. Their increasing knowledge of phonics and of high-frequency words, and their growing repertoire of writing skills and strategies also means that they are coming closer to capturing stories that flow from their imaginations onto the page. You will teach them, then, to mine their lives for stories that matter and then to turn those stories into shapely narratives under the influence of finely crafted mentor texts.

This book stands on the shoulders of its predecessor, *Authors as Mentors* in Units of Study for Primary Writing. Those of you familiar with that book will recognize its spirit of inquiry and mentorship very much at play in this new version, now tailored to second-graders and almost completely rewritten. Rather than spotlighting multiple texts by particular authors, this book focuses on just two titles, each by a "master" author. That is, this is not a mentor author study so much as a close study of craft. Specifically, students will study how authors use craft to convey meaning.

You will share two demonstration texts with your students—Jane Yolen's luminous *Owl Moon* and Angela Johnson's deeply moving *The Leaving Morning* (the latter was also spotlighted in *Authors as Mentors*). These two books weave through six weeks of instruction, and they are worthy of such deep study. Each book brims with craft that children this age can recognize and

then replicate in their own writing—to their best seven- and eight-year-old ability. These texts also feature two very different families and very different small moments; it was important to us that they resonate with children of different backgrounds and yet feel universal.

Of course, the point isn't the content of these books so much as the ways their authors use craft to convey meaning. You could actually choose other books; the instruction is designed to be transferable across texts, just as it is transferable across units.

Meanwhile, our bigger goal is that the work children do positions them to be thoughtful writers—ones who write with purpose about topics that matter to them. You'll notice, throughout this book, then, that we teach children ways to write so as to bring out meaning—with the knowledge that children will grasp this to varying degrees and to the best of their second-grade ability. We introduce some big ideas early on, simply to lay the groundwork for what's to follow in ensuing years of writing workshop. After all, the curriculum we describe in this series—and have developed over many years at the Reading and Writing Project—is a spiral curriculum, which means that students will have many opportunities, in later grades, to practice using the craft moves we introduce this year—as well as others they acquire—with increasing sophistication and to greater effect.

Of course, even in the case of your most advanced writers, you won't expect that children will leave this unit writing perfectly crafted pieces. Children cannot create even rough approximations of well-crafted writing without a great deal of instruction and practice. But in this unit, children can draw on their backpack of tools for writing narratives in general and small moments in particular, using those tools to draft stories that readers are eager to read. Whereas in first grade, the emphasis in the opening unit is on bringing characters to life by making them move and talk, think and feel, now students will also draw on simple craft moves, such as using precise words to make their writing more specific or beautiful.

Across the unit, children will add to this repertoire, learning ways that authors draw on their senses to describe what they see, feel, hear, and so on, to make readers feel like they are there, in the story, or learning to write in ways that lead readers to hope that something happens in the story or to create a beautiful image or spotlight a strong feeling. Students will learn ways to orient readers by establishing a clear setting and situation. Your job will be to inspire your second-grade writers to create the types of narratives that read like real literature, stories that published authors themselves would craft, while accepting their second-grade best. "You, too, can be master writers," you'll say, and by the end of the unit you'll celebrate your youngsters as such.

As with other writing units, your second-graders will also spend time learning to write by reading. Of course, the reading-writing connections they make in this unit are particularly pointed toward growing their skills in both capacities, because this unit is a mentor text study; that is, children will study craft moves as *readers* and then try them out as *writers*. Perhaps the area of reading, above all then, is where you'll find that this unit challenges children. We want to reiterate, again, that this is merely an introduction for your young students to work that they will be doing again and again, both this year and in years to follow. But do keep in mind that second-graders aren't entirely little kids—and their energy for trying new challenges is boundless. Children this age are eager to try again and again to get something just right, so a good portion of this book focuses on the work of revision.

This unit is also designed to support your second-graders' growing skills in the conventions of writing and their ability to communicate as members of a community—or partnership—listening and speaking in turn. The more practice you give your students to discuss books and their own writing with one another, the better chance you will have of setting them up to present themselves, their work, and their ideas to the world, not just in this one unit, but in life.

OVERVIEW OF THE UNIT

"Writers," you'll say to your children early in the unit. "I bet you're wondering how Jane Yolen and Angela Johnson came up with the ideas for their books, *Owl Moon* and *The Leaving Morning*. Maybe, in the middle of their regular lives, Jane and Angela grabbed hold of particular moments, moments that stayed with them, ones that got them thinking, 'Hey, I could write a story about that,' and then let those moments spark ideas for their stories." You can then say, "Starting today, each one of you is going to live like these 'master' writers, finding small moment ideas in your own lives and recording them on Tiny Topics notepads, just as Jane probably did, in the middle of the night, and as Angela probably did, in the middle of a big move." Over the course of Bend I, then, you will teach your students ways to stretch out and magnify their small moments, writing these with great attention to detail and to crafting powerful beginnings and endings. The bend ends with a day of goal setting, during which children can use the narrative checklist to assess their work and to set goals for themselves as writers.

In the next bend, you will spotlight writing with purpose and learning from authors' craft. You'll begin this bend by asking children to name their intentions as writers—what they hope their readers will feel—and revising on the go toward these. On the second day, you'll lead children in an inquiry into what makes *Owl Moon* so powerful; together, the class will examine a couple parts closely to consider what effect these have on readers and how the author has achieved that effect. Then students will try out these craft moves in their own writing. As the bend progresses, the emphasis shifts to understanding why an author would use a particular craft move, and children will revise with that in mind, paying attention, too, to word choice and language.

The final bend sets children up to make reading and writing connections, drawing on everything they have learned up until this point to discover craft moves in books they are reading on their own and to apply these to their own writing. There are two main goals in this bend: first, students will work with increasing independence, transferring what they have learned under your guidance and through shared inquiry to work that is now largely self-initiated. Second, children will devote careful attention to revision and editing, aiming to make their writing as clear and as powerful as it can be. The bend ends with a celebration in which you introduce your new class of "master writers" to their audience.

ASSESSMENT

World-class standards require that students develop some proficiency at writing three kinds of texts: opinion writing, informational writing, and narrative texts. We recommend, then, that you begin the year by giving children initial assessments in these three genres. Over the course of the year, you'll be able to measure children's growth against these initial writing tasks, which you may opt to repeat periodically, during relevant units, and certainly at the end of the year in the form of a summative assessment.

Before you begin teaching this unit, you can use the pieces of writing both to assess your new class of students and to inform your teaching plans for this first unit of study. Most likely, many of your students will be at level 1, which sets them up to work toward level 2 on the Narrative Writing Learning Progression found in the *Writing Pathways: Performance Assessments and Learning Progressions, K–5* book. That will mean that by the end of second grade, they'll be aligned to the expectations that most state standards set forth.

Of course, you will want to assess not only what your children can do on Day One and as they leave your room, but how they progress across the year. That is, you will want to have a sense of how each child learns, of how he or she moves across a variety of skill sets, acquiring increased proficiency in writing, speaking, and listening.

For the initial narrative writing task, for assessment, give your children a four-page booklet and ask them to write a story about something they have done. We recommend using the following prompt from the *Writing Pathways: Performance Assessments and Learning Progressions, K–5* book to start them off:

"I'm really eager to understand what you can do as writers of narratives, of stories, so today, will you please write the best personal narrative, the best Small Moment story, that you can write. Make this be the story of one time in your life. You might focus on just a scene or two. You'll have only forty-five minutes to write this true story, so you'll need to plan, draft, revise, and edit in one sitting. Write in a way that allows you to show off all you know about narrative writing.

"In your writing, make sure you:
- Make a beginning for your story
- Show what happened, in order
- Use details to help readers picture your story
- Make an ending for your story."

When children are done, collect their pieces to see what they produced, using the Narrative Writing Learning Progression to determine a starting level for each child. This will inform what you teach in terms of structure, elaboration, craft, cohesion, and meaning.

Many teachers duplicate their students' on-demand narratives for students to keep inside their writing folders. These initial pieces of writing can then serve as reminders to students of the level of work they were able to do at the start of the year. Meanwhile, students can measure any subsequent writing they do during this unit (and year) against this first piece, striving always to do better.

You can use this first writing task to assess where the bulk of your class falls, to inform your instruction for this first unit. You'll also see where each student falls in the Narrative Writing Learning Progression by comparing these initial pieces to the exemplar texts and then reading the specific descriptors to determine concrete next steps for each child. Note that no one piece will match a checklist in its entirety; a piece can be at level 1 even if a category or two don't add up.

Use the level descriptors to suggest next steps to individual students. You might say, for example, "You used to develop the people in your stories by . . . ," and read the descriptors from the prior level, "but now you are . . . ," and read the level 1 descriptor. "Here's one way to make your writing even better! You can . . . ," and read from the level 2 descriptor. You might even say, "Let me show you an example," and then cite a section of the level 2 exemplar text.

As the unit progresses, of course, you can expect that not all students will progress at the same rate, while nonetheless holding in mind certain year-end grade goals. Your goal is that by the end of this year, students will be able to craft focused, small moment narratives that depict several linked scenes and are elaborated with some dialogue, thoughts, and feelings. Second-graders should demonstrate an increasing use of craft moves and detail—sometimes at the cost of clarity. Expect that they'll introduce their stories with an initiating action, establish a setting, and end their pieces with a sense of closure. Meanwhile, their writing should display a growing understanding of grammar conventions. As you review the narrative writing assessments your children submit and consider your instruction for this first unit, keep an eye on these year-long goals.

GETTING READY

As you prepare for this unit, you will need to select two mentor texts that will be front and center during your instruction. We chose Jane Yolen's *Owl Moon* (featured largely in Bends I and II) and Angela Johnson's *The Leaving Morning* (featured largely in Bend III) and offer detailed teaching plans throughout this book that show you ways you and your students might explore the craft moves in each one. You might choose other texts, of course. What matters especially is that you use texts whose pages include the kind of craft you hope children will both notice and admire and also find success replicating in their own writing. To that end, we suggest you read your mentor texts again and again before beginning the unit, mining them for any craft moves you intend to explicitly teach, as well as for ones you will guide children to "discover" on their own. Read these like a reader first, enjoying the sounds and rhythm of each story and the feelings they inspire. Then pick up a stack of Post-its® and read these stories as a writer, noting what, exactly, each author does to create such powerful texts. Over the course of the unit, you and your students will do this same kind of careful reading and rereading, so you will be preparing for that work.

In addition to the two mentor texts you select for use during your minilessons, you'll want to fill your library with a variety of narratives that span your children's just-right reading levels. These should be stories that feel accessible to children both as readers and as writers, so that as children pore over them, studying craft, they will think to themselves, "What a great story! I could write one like that!" And then they will draw on that inspiration to write stories whose craft (not content) mimics that of these mentor texts.

Beginning on Day Two, children will carry around Tiny Topics notepads (two- by one-inch spiral notepads) to record anything from their lives that sparks story ideas. You'll keep one of your own and will bring it with you to school, with ideas for stories you'll share with the class. This means, of course, that you'll need to have in mind possible stories from your own life that you can use to model, one for each bend. You'll grow these over the course of each bend to show children how to turn ideas for writing into deliberately crafted pieces of literature.

Occasionally we incorporate objects in our lessons—usually to drive home a metaphor we hope will illuminate the day's teaching. For example, we bring seashells and magnifying glasses in on Day Four to signify the work of looking at something closely to describe it in detail. You might use entirely different objects (or none at all). The idea is simply to help clarify any potentially obscure teaching.

Finally, you'll need to have on hand the writing supplies children will use over the course of this unit: different kinds of paper, pens, markers, writing folders, and anything else you might imagine incorporating into this narrative writing unit.

ONLINE DIGITAL RESOURCES

A variety of resources to accompany this and the other Grade 2 Units of Study in Opinion, Information, and Narrative Writing are available in the online resources. To access and download all the digital resources for this grade-level set:

1. Go to **www.heinemann.com** and click the link in the upper right to log in. (If you do not have an account yet, you will need to create one.)

2. **Enter the following registration code** in the box to register your product: **WUOS_GR2**

3. Enter the security information requested, obtained from within your unit book.

4. Once you have registered your product it will appear in the list of "View my registered Online Resources, Videos, and eBooks." (Note: You only need register once; then each time you return to your account, just click the "My Online Resources" link to access these materials.)

(You may keep copies of these resources on up to six of your own computers or devices. By downloading the files you acknowledge that they are for your individual or classroom use and that neither the resources nor the product code will be distributed or shared.)

OWL
MOON

Discovering Small Moments That Matter

Generating Ideas for Writing

IN THIS SESSION, you'll teach children that one way they can learn to write meaningful, beautiful stories is to study the craft of mentor authors.

GETTING READY

- Plan to start your minilesson before children gather in the meeting area.

- Writing center, set up to include five-page booklets, single sheets of paper, revision strips and flaps, and writing caddies with pens, staplers, Post-it® notes, and date stamps

- A preassigned table monitor for each table in your room (see Connection)

- *Owl Moon* by Jane Yolen and *The Leaving Morning* by Angela Johnson or other mentor texts that show writerly craft (see Teaching)

- A Jane Yolen quotation (see Teaching)

- Your own Tiny Topics spiral notepad, 2″ × 1″, with Small Moment ideas already written, or in mind to share with the class (see Teaching and Active Engagement)

- Writing folders, one for each student, with a red dot on one side, for finished pieces, and a green dot on the other side, for in-process pieces (see Share)

- Mentor texts and anchor charts from previous year (see Share)

- Piece of student writing from the day (see Share)

THIS SESSION REPRESENTS the official launch of your second-grade writing workshop. You will want to create ribbon-cutting excitement, so that children feel as if they are embarking on a whole new chapter in their writing lives—because they are! The difference between the little kids who graduated first grade and the big ones who now return as second-graders is enormous. It can sometimes feel as if in two short months they have done a whole year's worth of growing up. Entering second-graders express themselves with greater precision and confidence, they have a new awareness of the world outside themselves, and the stories they tell feel richer. You will want to capitalize on this in your writing workshop.

Remind your students of all they learned to do last year in Small Moment writing, and tell them that because of this learning, they are ready for more sophisticated writing work—they are ready to learn from the masters. "Master writers," you'll say, "don't just tell *any* stories; they tell *meaningful* ones. Master writers create powerful books that people across the world read again and again and again." Then read just the opening lines of each of the two mentor texts the class will study in this unit—we recommend *Owl Moon* by Jane Yolen and *The Leaving Morning* by Angela Johnson, two beautifully crafted picture books—and marvel at how the openings alone carry such weight.

Then turn the reins over to your students. Suggest that the class conduct an inquiry. Say, "I wonder how these two authors came up with their ideas—what do you think?" and see what ideas children generate. Hopefully they'll recognize that both Jane and Angela chose to write about memorable moments—ones that stood out from everyday life. Help students realize that these authors have experienced moments that made them think, "There's a powerful story here"—and that children have had those moments, too. That is, you'll aim to convey not only that Jane and Angela are masterful writers, but that children can learn to write in similar ways. You will want your children to adore these two writers and also to identify with them.

"*Second-graders express themselves with greater precision and confidence, they have a new awareness of the world outside themselves, and the stories they tell feel richer.*"

You'll want your students to take something else from this first day. You'll want them to understand that Jane and Angela didn't just come up with a story and "poof!" write it down. They had a process. Suggest that perhaps they carried little story idea notebooks (or Tiny Topics notepads, as you'll call them), in which they jotted ideas as these occurred to them. Tomorrow you'll give each student his or her very own Tiny Topics notepad. For now, you'll set children up to think in partnerships about moments from their own lives that matter enormously to them. Then you'll send them off to write, write, write!

Discovering Small Moments That Matter

Generating Ideas for Writing

CONNECTION

Remind children of the materials and routines of writing workshop and give them a chance to practice gathering.

Children were seated at their tables—not in the meeting area—as I began today's writing workshop. "Second-graders, it's time for writing workshop. Just like in first grade, every day we will have time set aside to work on writing projects. At the end of each unit, we will then publish our final products. Do you remember how you all had writing celebrations last year? Remember when you read your work to an audience and received all that wonderful feedback? I remember. I attended a few at the end of the year! You all wrote *so* much and took such pride and care in making those published pieces. This year, we are going to do the same thing!"

I walked over to where I had set up our writing center, to the various baskets of paper, caddies with tools, and baskets of books that students had read and used last year as mentor texts. "This is our writing center. You will see that there are booklets and single sheets, strips and flaps, books you studied last year, and writing caddies." I held up an example of each of these. "These caddies are filled with pens, staplers, Post-it® notes, date stamps, and one folder for each of you—with your name at the top!

"Today, we begin our first unit of study! I have selected six of you to be table monitors." I gestured to a list names.

"Your job is to collect the caddies, place them on the table, and distribute the folders to each table where your new classmates sit. Over the next week, we will switch this job around, so that you all can practice it. Later, we will decide on class jobs for the next couple of months. For now, let's practice getting ready. Table monitors, set up the writing materials. Second-graders, gather in the meeting area, quickly and"—I gave a dramatic pause and almost whispered—"quietly."

Notice that children aren't yet in the meeting area when this teaching begins. That would have been easy to miss until midway into this minilesson, a reminder that you need to read a minilesson entirely through before teaching it.

It is essential that children transfer all they learned from a preceding year into this new writing workshop. We hope, therefore, that your teaching reminds children of what they've already learned to do and conveys that they enter this new year already poised to learn and do yet more. We recognize, however, that you'll alter this introduction if most of your children didn't have opportunities to write when they were in first grade.

Create a drumroll around this unit and remind students of all they learned about writing stories last year.

Once children were seated with their eyes on me, I said, "Do you know that I've been counting down the days of summer thinking about this moment? And now here it is—the start of your lives as second-grade writers! We are going to do some really special work to launch this year."

Leaning in I said, "We are going to learn from *master* writers. That means writers who stand out even among other published writers. Writers whose books are so powerful, so moving, and so beautifully crafted that people from all over the world read them again and again and again.

"Your teachers from last year told me that you *already* know how to write Small Moment stories about things that have happened to you. And they said that you also already know how to tell the exact actions the people in your stories make—*and* what they are thinking and feeling." I looked incredulous and said, "Is that true?" The kids nodded.

"Your teachers also told me that you learned how to do some things that professional writers do to fancy up their writing, like write three dots to build excitement, and write exciting parts with big bold words so that readers use a big, bold voice to read them. I couldn't believe it. I told those teachers, 'No way did first-graders do that!'" The kids were already on their knees, protesting that in fact they *had* tried out these craft moves last year.

"Is that right? In that case, I'm *certain* you're ready to learn from the masters. Are you game to try?" They nodded vigorously.

❖ **Name the teaching point.**

"Today, I want to teach you that master authors don't just tell *any* stories. They tell *meaningful* stories. Paying attention to the kinds of stories they choose to tell can inspire you when you are trying to come up with your own meaningful stories."

TEACHING

Introduce children to the master writers they will be studying, and read the beginning of a book by each one, pointing out how each story topic matters to its writer.

"Look at this, writers," I said, holding up Jane Yolen's book, *Owl Moon*, as if it were gold. "This book was written by a master writer named Jane Yolen. It's called *Owl Moon* and it's about a time when Jane's daughter, Heidi, went looking for owls late one night with her father." I leafed through the pages and said, "Jane felt that this one small moment was so special—this one owling trip that her husband and daughter shared in the woods—that she stretched it out across all these pages." I leafed through the book to show kids. "We're going to read this book together later. I'll just read the beginning of it now. As I do, listen to how Jane shows us how special this moment was."

You'll alter this so that it matches whatever you believe your children did learn during the preceding year. It may not yet be the case in your school that teachers across a grade teach in ways that are shared, allowing you to count on your children bringing a background to second grade. But hopefully your school is working toward that goal. The world-class standards convey a very strong message to all of us: we can't bring students to high levels of achievement if we can never count on any prior instruction. And, yes, it does take a village to raise a child!

It was late one winter night, long past my bedtime, when Pa and I went owling. There was no wind. The trees stood still as giant statues. And the moon was so bright the sky seemed to shine. Somewhere behind us a train whistle blew, long and low, like a sad, sad song.

"Isn't that beautiful, writers? See how quiet and bright that night was, and how precisely Jane describes it? From just those opening lines we can already tell how special that particular experience was.

"I want to show you another book. Listen to the first line from this book, called *The Leaving Morning*. Angela Johnson wrote this one. It's a story about when her family moved. Listen to how it begins."

The LEAVING happened on a soupy, misty morning, when you could hear the street sweeper. Sssshhhshsh.

Notice that you can cup your hands around tiny segments of a text, reading a line or two aloud, to make your point. It's rare for you to do large swatches of read-aloud within a minilesson.

"The *Leaving*. Isn't that an unusual way to describe a moving day? Like Jane, Angela uses images and sounds to bring her first page to life—and you can tell that this day left its mark on her.

"Writers, do you see how carefully these two master writers worded their opening lines? Even without hearing the rest of their books, it's so clear that these small moments have BIG meaning for these authors, isn't it?"

This is a long minilesson already, so resist the temptation to go on and on. Brevity is important.

Brainstorm with your children possible ways that Jane Yolen and Angela Johnson—and any author—might come up with a Small Moment story that matters.

"I wonder how these two authors came up with their ideas. Jane, for example. How did she imagine a story about her husband taking their daughter owling one night? And Angela—what do you think made her write about the 'Leaving'? Hmm, . . . Turn and tell the person sitting next to you what you think."

After a couple of minutes, I reconvened the group. "Writers, I could tell you were thinking really hard just now, trying to figure out how these writers came up with their ideas. Some of you noticed that both authors recorded things that happened to them, or that happened to people they know. That's definitely one way authors get ideas. Some of you noticed, too, that these aren't just everyday moments. Angela didn't write about any ol' morning, and Jane didn't write about any ol' night. Angela and Jane picked moments that stood out from everyday ones. Maybe in the middle of their regular lives, they grabbed hold of moments that stayed with them, moments that got them thinking, 'Hey, I could write a story about that.' For years, people have tried to figure out what makes a good story. Jane Yolen once said, 'I like books that touch my head and my heart at the same time' (janeyolen.com)." As I said this, I touched my head and heart. "That's powerful, right? Books that make you think *and* feel?"

Your children will not all have the chance to talk, and they surely won't finish talking before the turn-and-talk time is over. Your goal is to ignite a certain kind of involvement, and just two minutes of talk accomplishes that goal.

Suggest that Jane Yolen and Angela Johnson may use a notepad to record the little details that later become stories.

"Small moment ideas occur to writers all the time—so writers know that they need to be prepared to get an idea down on paper, even if there isn't time to write the whole story right then and there. Maybe Jane overheard her husband and daughter slip out of bed to go owling in the middle of the night, and she was too sleepy to write that story, so she just wrote the idea in a Tiny Topics notepad like this." I held up a tiny spiral notepad. "Maybe she wrote 'David and

It takes imagination for the author study to inform children's work because all we have to go on is the author's final text, not the author's process. This allows you to imagine the author doing whatever you want your kids to do! I emphasize the lifework of writing not because of our study of Angela Johnson and Jane Yolen, in particular, but because by second grade, children are ready to have meaningful, wide-awake writing lives. We use the author study, then, as a forum for teaching that writers live differently.

Heidi—up in the night.' And I'm sure Angela didn't have time to write about her family's move in the middle of packing everything up! So she probably grabbed her Tiny Topics notepad and just quickly jotted, 'The Leaving.'"

ACTIVE ENGAGEMENT

Share your tiny notepad ideas with children. Then ask them to think of a Small Moment story idea and to tell that topic to the person sitting next to them. Suggest that they try to name why this moment matters.

"Writers, last night I tried to do what Jane and Angela and so many writers do. I sat in my favorite chair and thought about little moments that stood out for me—ones I might want to write about. Bit by bit, ideas crept in. Like one time when I was your age and I got a big role in the class play. I was so scared, I didn't think I had it in me to get on that stage—but then I did it! And I felt proud. I thought to myself, 'Yes, there is a story there that I might tell,' and I grabbed hold of it.

"Right now, think of a small moment that's happened in your life—one that stands out from all everyday moments—and tell that idea to your partner. See if you can also say why that moment matters. When it's your turn to listen, be the kind of listener who cares. Ask for more information if you don't yet understand why this moment was so special."

I gave children a minute to talk, and listened in to their conversations. Isabelle said to Jordan, "I can write about how, when I went skating, the ice was slippery. I almost fell. My sister held my hand." She gestured to show how her out-stretched arms helped her maintain her balance while skating.

Isabelle acted like she was done and Jordan said, "So why was that moment special?" I gave him a thumbs up.

"Um, 'cause I was proud that I didn't fall. And my sister helped me," Isabelle said.

"I'm going to write about when I was with my dad in the park and I was trying to knock icicles down from the trees," Jordan said.

"Did you get any icicles?" Isabelle asked, but before Jordan could answer, it was time to reconvene the class.

Whispering, Jordan said, "Yeah, 'cause my dad put me on his shoulders! Then I could reach."

Ask writers to get started by telling the beginning of one story to their partner.

"Writers, I'm hearing such wonderful ideas about small moments that have happened in your own lives—ones that stand out to you from your everyday lives. I don't want you to lose any momentum, so right now, turn again to the person sitting next to you, and try out a story beginning. See if you can start your story in a way that shows the reader just how special this moment was to you. Turn and start to story-tell!"

Notice, here, that as you position students to try out the strategy and generate topics for writing, you can simultaneously teach them about being good listening partners. You might, for example, ask students to listen to and extend each other's thoughts just by asking the question "Why?" This allows each writer to reflect on his or her topic a bit more, focusing on meaning. Teaching students to respond to one another in this way gives them a concrete model of how to work together to extend and focus their ideas. In the long term, this will be a supportive structure in improving both your writers and their writing.

LINK

Remind children that master writers can influence them. Direct them to begin writing and, as they work, name aloud the ways they do so efficiently.

After just a moment, I interrupted so children would still have energy to tell their stories in writing. "Authors can be so inspirational! They influence our own ideas, they fill us with beautiful language, they remind us why we love to read and write! For the next few weeks, you are going to mentor yourselves to authors and learn from books, as if they are your teachers!

"This year, because you are older and wiser, not only will you get straight to your writing, but you will also craft powerful literature, just like the authors whose books line our shelves. Writers, who is ready to begin? If you have an idea, you can stand up, walk to the writing center, get paper, and then head to your table—quickly and quietly." No one moved. Without talking, I leaned down toward the students gathered closest to me, nodded, and motioned to the writing center, "Why don't you all go ahead, and we will watch you get started."

"There goes April. She is walking to the center and picking a five-page booklet! Now she is headed to her table. There goes Mohammed. He is already at his table and what is he doing? Looks like he is taking out a pen and starting to write his name. Yes, that is what he is doing. Will he take the date stamp next? Yes! He remembers! And look over here." I walked over to another table. "Rocio has already started writing. She remembers, too! Who else remembers? If you have an idea, place your thumb on your knee. When I wave my hand over your head you can get up and get started—quickly and quietly."

You will want to decide how the author you have selected can help children with the very beginning of their writing process. You won't want to say, "Jane Yolen wrote about her daughter owling with her dad and you can write about something you did with your dad, too," because you are hoping children learn strategies (not topics) from authors they admire. You could help children emulate Jane's process of mining her life for topics. I decided to focus not on helping children know what they could write about, but on reminding them to zoom in on tiny, specific topics.

Cultivating Independent Writers

T HE FIRST DAYS OF WORKSHOP will tell your students everything—these early days set the tone and expectation for the whole year. You will want to make sure you are providing a rigorous workshop that also inspires and motivates. Working with your students in one-to-one conferences and small groups will be crucial. When does one start these conversations? Right at the very beginning.

Initially, you can anticipate that students will need reminders about ways to solve problems on their own. Remind them of ways to figure out hard words, how to start a new piece when they are done, how to use sketches to realize what else to write, or how to keep their conversations in support of their writing.

During the first week of workshop, you may want to make your conferences very quick, or work with whole tables at one time. This not only allows you to keep the workshop flowing, but also gives you the chance to meet and talk with all your students a few times during the week. You can also use the on-demand assessment that you did prior to the beginning of the unit to prioritize conferences and to set up small groups.

In one-to-one conferences you hold the first week of workshop, you will want to notice what each student is doing as a writer. Read a student's writing, carefully and ask a few quick questions. While you will already have a sense of the writer from the on-demand assessment, you can learn more from these short conversations. You might inquire about how the student got her idea for a story, what **IMPORTANT!** are next when she finishes the page or the piece, or how she chose the details that are on the page. When you ask children about their process as they work, you will see which students are aware of the strategies they are using and which ones need the strategies named, so that they can draw on and reference these in the future. Naming what a student has done and reminding that child to use that strategy again in other places or pieces is a powerful move. It conveys the expectation that writers reuse skills again and again, and positions students to do likewise, often in deeper, more nuanced ways.

MID-WORKSHOP TEACHING
Finding Meaning in Everyday Moments

As students were working, I called for their attention. "Writers, some of you have told me that you can't think of any special moments in your lives. All you can think of are things you do every day, like eat and play. That got me thinking: meaningful moments are sometimes ordinary! Remember *Night of the Veggie Monster*? The book you read last year about the little boy who dreaded eating vegetables? George McClements (2008) was inspired by his picky-eater son to write that story. And what a great story! But it was about something meaningful that happened during an everyday dinner. Remember? His son realized, after all that fuss, that the pea wasn't so bad after all! Each one of you has lots of moments like that. You might want to thumb through books on our shelves to see if they spark ideas. Of course, you won't take those writers' exact story ideas—just like you won't take Jane's story about owling, or Angela's about 'The Leaving.' But you might find that these stories remind you of moments in your *own* lives worth writing about."

Often, in addition to conferring with individuals and small groups, you will voice over during the workshop time, to encourage stamina. You might say things like, "Wow, this room really *sounds* like a room of writers! Keep your pens moving!" Or, "I see someone starting a new piece, because she has finished her first story. All of you can do that." These voiceovers—comments that narrate and name the positive things happening in the workshop—not only give little minor teaching tips but also give the room energy!

In these ways, you will begin to build a highly motivating environment, one that welcomes your second-graders to this new, rigorous year.

Organizing Ongoing and Finished Writing Projects

Introduce writing folders to the class, explaining that one pocket is for writing that is finished and one is for writing that is ongoing.

"Writers," I called out from the middle of the classroom, holding up multicolored folders. "I have something for your writing! A treasure chest of sorts! Just like last year, this year you will keep all of your writing in a folder with two pockets. Does anyone remember how to use these two sides?"

"I remember!" April called out. "Stop and go!"

"That's right. This side," I pointed to the green-dot side, "is your 'Go!' side. It is the side for pieces you are still working on. This side," I pointed to the red-dot side, "is the 'Stop!' side. It is the side for work that is done.

"I am going to give each of you your own folder. Will you do two things? First, decide whether your writing goes on the green-dot side or the red-dot side and put it inside the folder. Second, label the green-dot and red-dot sides with words that show what they are to help you remember. You might write 'Go' and 'Stop' or 'Still working' and 'Feels like I finished,' or 'Ongoing work' and 'Finished work.' You decide.

"Once you're done labeling each side of your folder, bring it to the rug with you."

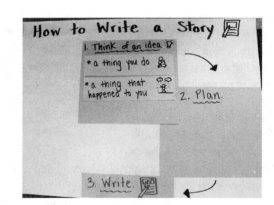

Share writing from today's workshop that reflects last year's teaching and elicit children's responses.

I revealed some charts and mentor texts from last year that I had placed on the blackboard tray, in a display. As children gathered on the rug, I gave them a moment to exclaim over these. "I'm going to read a few of the pieces you wrote today. As I do so, will you notice some things from last year's teaching that your classmates have done to make their Small Moment stories the best they could be? These charts and books can remind you of what you learned last year.

Make a fuss as you pass out the writing folders, reminding students of the special care writers take to keep their writing safe. These folders will become an important tool for them this year, as they have been in previous years, so make sure you take the time to review how they will work.

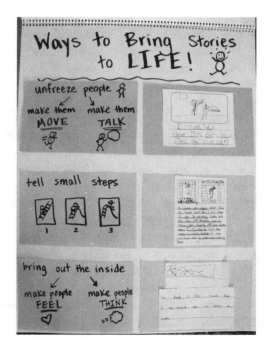

"Listen to the first page of Fabiha's story. (See Figure 1–1.) Notice what she remembered to do from the first-grade chart when telling her small moment." I read just one page of Fabiha's writing.

> One bright sunny day, me and my brother were
> playing in the Xbox. "I'm bored," I said
> lying down on the bed. "Me too," my brother
> said. "I wish we had something else to do" I said.

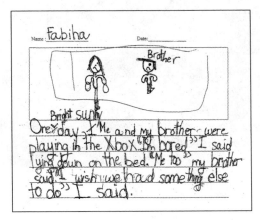

FIG. 1–1 This first page of Fabiha's Small Moment story shows how she added a variety of details to stretch out the beginning.

"So what do you see on our chart that Fabiha remembered to include?" To give children some support, I ran my pen under the quotation marks, the words *One bright sunny day*, and under the action words. "Turn and tell your partner what you notice—more than one thing!" I gave children a moment to reflect.

"She made people talk in her story," Grace said.

"She told what people did. She said that they were playing on the Xbox," Brandon said. "And lying on the bed!"

"She told us the setting!" Stephen called out.

Encourage students to draw on last year's instruction as they write.

"Fantastic observations. I know you might be thinking, 'I forgot to do those things in my story!' Don't worry, writers, we will have workshop time every day, just like you had in kindergarten and first grade, so you can work on your stories. Tomorrow you can revise your work to include some of the things you noticed here, and when you start new pieces, you won't forget these moves that make small moments so powerful!

"Writers, quickly and quietly get up from your spots on the rug, go back to your tables, and put your treasure chest of writing in your caddies, at your tables. Table monitors, can you please make sure that you take all the writing materials to the writing center? Off you go!"

Capturing Story Ideas
Tiny Topics Notepads

IN THIS SESSION, you'll teach children that writers capture everyday moments and save them as possible story ideas to write later.

GETTING READY

✔ Two Jane Yolen quotations (see Connection and Share)

✔ 2″ × 1″ Tiny Topics notepads, one for each child; buy spirals and cut them in thirds (see Connection)

✔ Your Tiny Topics notepad (see Teaching)

✔ A pen for the Active Engagement of the minilesson

✔ Construction paper that will fit neatly on the covers of the Tiny Topics notepads; write each child's name on a cover and paper-clip these onto the spiral notebooks; have extras on hand (see Share)

✔ A couple of student examples (Share)

✔ *Owl Moon* by Jane Yolen, to be read in its entirety after this second session and before Session 3, during read-aloud

PROFESSIONAL WRITERS KNOW the importance of keeping a small notebook on hand wherever they go because they know that an idea can strike at any moment—and that it can just as easily be forgotten. Today, you'll give each child his or her very own Tiny Topics notepad so that they, too, can capture their ideas as they occur. This may seem like small business—and it's true that today's teaching is relatively simple—but you'll convey two important messages through it.

The first is that story ideas live all around us, in the smallest moments and objects. Ideas are in the details of life, in the ladybug that lands on your finger, the touch of your grandmother's hands, the grin on the new kid's face when she gives you a turn on the swings. Ideas that lead to powerful stories often stem from the tiniest things—if you slow down and take note of them.

The second message is that people who notice the details and imagine ways to spin these into stories live differently. They live as writers. "From today on," you'll say, "you'll live differently because you'll become the kind of person who doesn't just turn into a writer during writing workshop, but who lives *life* as a writer. You'll wake up as a writer, eat breakfast as a writer, walk to school as a writer, go to bed as a writer—everywhere you go and everything you do from this day on you will do as a writer." The notepad will embody this new emphasis on living wide-awake, attentive lives, like real authors.

The hope is that today's teaching will inspire a flurry of ideas, and that children will find significance in observations of their own, unprompted. However, if you think your particular class of students will need additional scaffolding, you might remind children of the strategies for generating ideas that they learned last year: thinking about things that they have done or that have happened to them, or of times they had strong feelings.

Of course, you won't want children to spend the entire workshop finding and jotting ideas in their notepads. You'll share the kinds of details you notice and show your class how you quickly jot just a few words as a reminder to yourself, and then pick one to write about. You'll give children a chance to practice this themselves before sending them off to write.

Capturing Story Ideas
Tiny Topics Notepads

CONNECTION

Ask table monitors to set up workshop and, meanwhile, convene writers.

"Table monitors, remember where the caddies are? Folders and writing tools? Please set up workshop for us. Everyone, come to the meeting area with a pen. There is something special waiting for you at your rug spot. I know you may be tempted to take a look at it and investigate, but if you wait just a few minutes, I'll explain to you exactly what it is."

Prior to students gathering in the meeting area, I had set out Tiny Topics notepads on each of their rug spots.

Remind students to watch for little things that could become stories and to record these in their Tiny Topics notepads.

I read aloud the quotation I'd written on chart paper, and credited the master author Jane Yolen (janeyolen.com).

> *"Every time I get an idea, I write it down and file it in my Idea File."*

"Writers, we need to keep 'idea files,' too. I was thinking you all might want to live writerly lives just like Jane, Angela, and other writers in the world. I've got something very special for each of you, right there on the rug in front of you!" I held up one of the tiny notepads. "This is a Tiny Topics notepad. It can be *your* 'idea file.' Yesterday, you learned that writers like Jane Yolen write with details because they live with details—you can, too! Writers find stories in the lost mitten—the walk in the rain—footprints in the snow—and they jot these details down to write out later."

Details convey worlds more than generalizations. Had I said simply, "Writers finds stories in small details," I wouldn't have stirred children's imaginations nearly as much as with the statement, "Writers find stories in the lost mitten—the walk in the rain—footprints in the snow...."

❧ **Name the teaching point.**

"Today, I want to teach you that just as writers collect tiny details that they can later turn into stories, you can do the same thing. You can do this at lunch, at home, on the playground—whenever you find a good idea or remember something you want to write, you can just jot it down."

TEACHING

Demonstrate getting an idea for a story from a tiny event and jotting it down to develop later.

"So, if you are out in the world or in school and come up with a great idea for a story, write it down for later! Let's practice a little, right here, right now. Let's in our minds take a little trip through our day so far, and see if a little detail sparks a story for us!

"I'll go first. Let me think about the day so far. Oh, I know! Earlier, I looked at those birds we heard singing outside our window. They were beautiful, but disrupting our reader's workshop! Remember? I could write that down in my tiny notepad. But I won't write down ALL those words. I'll just write a couple of words to hold on to that idea. I could write, 'birds singing' or 'birds disturbing us.' Either one will help me remember what my story is so that I can write about it later. I'm going to write, 'birds disturbing us.' Just three words." I opened my Tiny Topics notepad and wrote quickly in front of the children before holding it up for them to see.

"Did you see that? Did you see how I jotted just a quick, short reminder? But *what* I wrote will remind me about the story that I want to write."

ACTIVE ENGAGEMENT

Ask children to think back over their day to find a small moment that could become a story, then jot it down to write about later.

"Right here, before you write, give this a try. Do you have an idea for a future story? Are there things happening around this classroom that you could turn into one? Think across your day so far, and jot down one, two, or even more ideas in *your* Tiny Topics notepads." I gave children a minute of silence, knowing only some would use this time to write.

"Writers, may I stop you? Isabelle already wrote two things. On one page, she jotted, 'almost falling on the ice.' That's one tiny topic she could write about. On the next page, she wrote, 'too small coat' because last night she tried on her coat and the sleeves came to here on her"—I gestured to my elbow—"and she thought she could write about how that felt! If she decides to turn that into a story, will she write the whole story here, in her Tiny Topics notepad?"

"Noooooo!" the students chorused.

"You're right. She'd get a booklet like this"—I held up a five-page booklet from the writing center—"to write her whole story. Keep going—try to get one more idea!" I gave students thirty more seconds to do this.

Drawing on a shared class experience brings children into the demonstration teaching, making it more likely to stick.

Of course, not all the kids will grasp what to put into the notepads (a phrase capturing their topic idea, as in "knocking down icicles") versus the booklets (the Small Moment story, like those they've written all year). You may need to confer or lead strategy lessons to help kids who don't understand the difference.

Share the writing a few students did to help generate even more ideas.

"Let's hear from some others. What did you jot down on your notepad to turn into a story?" I invited the class to share out.

"'Purring on the chair' because my cat sleeps next to me," Ramon said.

"'Mom left,'" Grace said. "It's a story about when my mom left me in my class and she forgot to say good-bye to me."

"I wrote, 'cherry pie' and I can almost taste it right now!" Justin said.

I know that as children call out ideas, this will help stir the imaginations of those who need some support.

LINK

Convey that jotting down small moment story ideas is a habit that will serve children for a lifetime of writing.

"You are all thinking of so many moments that will make fabulous stories!" I said. "Today, tonight, tomorrow—and forever!—be on the lookout for the small things in your lives that could make memorable stories, and catch them! Write them down! Be like Jane Yolen; be a writer. Listen and look closely and don't let everything pass you by. You'll be able to write with details because you'll *live* with details. Start now!"

Remind writers of strategies they know to get an idea, and ask them to use those or other ideas to get started writing.

"Remember, if you don't have an idea yet for a story, you can do a few things as a writer." I used my fingers to list off the suggestions. "You can get inspiration from our books in the writing center; you can look at your Tiny Topics notepad for an idea that you jotted; or, you can spend a little time thinking about the details in this room or in your day, weekend, or life. Once you have a few ideas, start writing! Each of you is going to fill up your folder with stories. Good luck, writers. Off you go!"

Because this is early in a new unit, I want children to be inspired. I want them to believe, as I do, that there is something majestic about finding significance in the small moments of our lives and writing these as stories. I also want to spell out very concrete, doable strategies they can use today.

Supporting Elaboration Before and After Children Write

AS YOU CONFER WITH STUDENTS in the first few days of school, you will find that you will need to support some kids in saying more—either from the start or after they've written their story. If they haven't yet written the story, it helps to ask them to tell it to you. As I pulled up a chair next to Mallika, I began by asking her what her writing plan for the day was. She told me that her plan was to write about the supermarket, going shopping with her mom.

I pressed on, knowing the importance of hearing a child's plan for writing. "How will that story go, Mallika? I know you haven't written it, but how will you tell it?" If, as I listen to the child's story, it sounds like a sort of "laundry list" of actions, I tend to follow up by asking, "What made this time so memorable? What was the main thing that happened?" "I accidentally put the food in the wrong cart!" Mallika said.

"Really? That's so funny! What actually happened? Walk me through everything!" Generally, once children have had a chance to rehearse their stories a bit, the words flow more smoothly. By giving Mallika a chance to oral story-tell with me, I knew she'd be able to write faster and longer. I dictated her first words to her, waited as she wrote a few of them, and then left her to write (see Figure 2–1). When she came up for air, I said, "Mallika, do you realize that you wrote longer about this story and more quickly than ever? What worked for you today is something you can try from now on—you can always tell your story to a writing partner before you write. That kind of rehearsal works for many writers, and it certainly worked for you today! "

Of course, you won't always be able to talk to a child before the youngster embarks on a story, so there are times when your interaction will occur after a story is written.

MID-WORKSHOP TEACHING   Give Your Writing a Small Moment Check

"One, two, three, eyes on me," I chanted, from the middle of the classroom. No one stopped writing or chatting. I tried once more, "Writers!" Suddenly all the writers looked up from their tables. "One, two, three, all eyes on me!" I chanted again. "Thank you for looking at me! I have something I want to quickly teach you. When I need your attention, I am going to always sing, 'One, two, three, eyes on me.' And you all can chant back, 'One, two, eyes on you!' Shall we try it?" We practiced once more.

"There is one more thing that I want to teach you. Last year, you all wrote small moment stories. You wrote about tiny topics, small seed ideas. Remember, you didn't write about the big topic—the watermelon—you chose one small idea. Well, I have noticed that some of your stories are those *big* stories that seem to have lots of little seed stories in them—lots of tiny topics! This happens to me all the time. In fact, just the other day, instead of writing about just one small moment, I wrote about my whole trip to the beach. I wrote about going for a swim in the ocean with my friend Frances, looking for shells alone by the shore, and eating lunch on the sand. I need to pick just one of these moments to write about. I can jot down the others in my Tiny Topics notepad to write about another day. That gives me a whole lineup of stories to write! I can rip off the pages of this story and put them in the 'Work in Progress' side of my folder.

"Look at the story you are writing right now. Are you writing a story about a small moment, like my story about the birds singing, or is your story more similar to this beach story, that has lots of Tiny Topics inside of it? If you are writing about a lot of moments, pick just one and write down the extra story ideas in your notepad for a new day. Pull those pages off and put them into your folder. If you are writing a Small Moment story, keep going. Then, when you finish, just give it a double check! Give it the 'Small Moment' check."

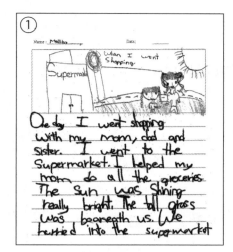

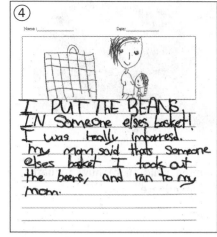

One day I went shopping with my mom, dad and sister. I went to the supermarket. I helped my mom do all the groceries. The sun was shining really bright. The tall grass was beneath us. We hurried into the supermarket.

My mom told me to put some food in a basket. The food was some okra beans. I held the okra beans in my hand and walked.

I went towards my basket. I was looking somewhere else. I didn't know what I was doing. So by accident . . .

I PUT THE BEANS IN someone else's basket! I was really embarrassed. My mom said, "That's someone else's basket." I took out the beans and ran to my mom.

FIG. 2–1 This piece shows how the writer, Mallika, stretched out her small moment across pages after she had an opportunity to rehearse it first. It also shows what Mallika remembers from first grade. She uses ellipses, some dialogue, and bold words for emphasis.

I watched Grace write quickly, one sentence on one page, another sentence on the next page, and another on the next. Her handwriting was larger than normal, and she was racing through each page. Midway through the fourth page (and the fourth line), I complimented Grace on finding a topic and turning it into a small moment, but then pressed to see if she had plans for revision. "So, can you tell me your plans for your story?" I leaned in closely.

"Well, I just wrote it. And now you can read it, and the kids can," Grace said as she packed the story away in her writing folder and closed the folder securely.

"Grace, I'm confused." I brought the story out and read it:

I thought my mom had left me.
I looked for her
And I couldn't find her.

And I looked some more.
And then
I found her.

"It doesn't look like you've gone back to revise your story yet. I would understand your quick dismissal of this story if it was one you didn't care about, but this sounds like one that really matters! And it took you about five seconds to write it! Don't you think it deserves more time?"

With a bit of nudging to see and say more, Grace said aloud what she saw in her mind's eye, and then added that to the page. Then I reminded her that writers imagine a story moment by moment, almost like a movie, to find and record the details their stories need.

Collecting Ideas for Small Moment Stories

Remind children of how to gather efficiently for the share portion of the workshop, and praise their independence.

"Writers, it's time to gather. Will you put your writing in your folders and place your folders and writing tools in the caddies? Hold onto your Tiny Topics notepads, though, and bring those to the meeting area with you. Table monitors, please clean up the writing, put everything in the writing center, and then come to the meeting area. Everyone else, join me in the meeting area, now, quickly and quietly.

When the children were all seated in the meeting area I said, "I saw that in workshop, you were all very busy writing. I even noticed that when some of you finished, you didn't just sit there, wondering what was going to happen next. Instead, you took out your Tiny Topics notepads and started collecting new story ideas. That is independence for you!"

Remind children of a strategy they can use when they are stuck. In this case, remind them they can look at and listen to the world around them for writing ideas.

"But sometimes, writing doesn't always go so smoothly, even for me. Sometimes, I feel stuck and wonder, 'What should I write about? I have nothing to say.' That will probably happen to you one of these days, too.

"So what can we do when we're stuck? Here's what one of our master writers—Jane Yolen—has to say. This is from her website:

> *I am always asked where I get my ideas from. That is a very difficult question to answer, since I get my ideas from everywhere: from things I hear and things I see, from books and songs and newspapers and paintings and conversations. (janeyolen.com)*

"She's wise, Jane! What an important reminder: Writers can get an idea from almost anything! Don't forget to look and listen all around you when you are trying to find what to write about.

"Right now, can you share with the person next to you what your idea was today and where it came from?" I listened in to children's conversations and shared a few examples, like Elizabeth's firefly story (see Figure 2–2).

"Before you go, listen because this is important. I'm going to give each one of you a cover for your Tiny Topics notepad. Tonight, find and note in your pad some small moments from your life, and also decorate this cover for your notepad so that it is your own. Don't forget! Tomorrow, you'll share more of the tiny topics you found!

"Right now, if you sit at table 1, will you please come and get your cover from me? Then you can put your cover and your Tiny Topics notepad in your cubby to take home tonight. If you sit at table 2, . . . "

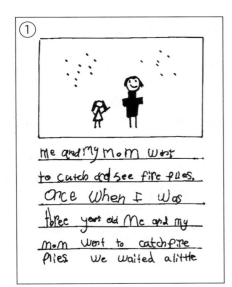

① Me and my mom went to catch and see fireflies. Once when I was three years old me and my mom went to catch fireflies. We waited a little

② until the fireflies came. Then we saw them! Their lights were glowing bright. My mom caught one. I tried to catch one also. Then suddenly I

③ caught one. I yelled out! Then we caught more and more. We would let them go each time we caught them. Then we would watch them

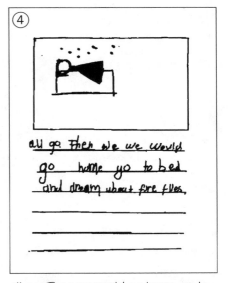

④ all go. Then we would go home, go to bed, and dream about fireflies.

FIG. 2–2   In Elizabeth's Small Moment story, she stretches the idea from her Tiny Topics notepad across pages, telling the reader what happened bit by bit.

Stretching Out Small Moments

IN THIS SESSION, you'll teach children what it looks and sounds like when writers tell the whole story of a tiny moment.

GETTING READY

✓ Students' Tiny Topics notepads and pencils (see Connection)

✓ Your own Tiny Topics notepad with details jotted on a few pages (see Teaching)

✓ Your own five-page booklet (see Teaching)

✓ Sharpened pencils, pens

✓ Scissors, tape, and staplers for revision

✓ Stapled booklets for writers, each containing four or five pages

✓ *Owl Moon* by Jane Yolen, or other mentor text, which you will have read with your class the day prior during your read-aloud (see Share)

✓ Post-it notes (see Share)

✓ Lanyards, or yarn, to turn the Tiny Topics notepads into necklaces (see Share)

TODAY'S TEACHING builds directly on what your students learned in the previous session. Children will come to school with tiny topics, tiny moments, inscribed in their notepads. Your challenge will be to help them turn these jotted notes into well-structured Small Moment stories. Last year, if your students were in a writing workshop, they will have had ample opportunity to practice Small Moment stories. Today, you will quickly remind them of the lessons they learned during their Small Moment and Fiction study: how to plan for how their stories will unfold across a series of pages, to write focused narratives, and to write with details. Then you will introduce two new elements to the planning work children will try out today. You will teach them that writers often record a few key words at the top of each page as reminders of what will go on that page, and you will teach them how to plan each *portion* of a story. Specifically, you will teach that just as a story has a beginning, middle, and end, so too does each of a story's parts. In this way, then, you add to children's writing-planning repertoire while also increasing the level of sophistication with which they plan—and the degree of detail and elaboration with which they will soon write.

Before today's minilesson, it will be important to have read *Owl Moon* to the class at least once, and preferably the day before, during read-aloud so that it is fresh in children's minds. Today, when you reread it, talk with the class about what Jane Yolen may have written down as she planned for writing this story.

In the teaching portion of this session, you will demonstrate telling your own story across your fingers, jotting a few key words on each page of a booklet, and then you will show how to plan the beginning, middle, and end of just one part of your own story. You'll offer children a chance to try this work themselves, in partnerships, before they go off to write.

Stretching Out Small Moments

CONNECTION

Match children with long-term writing partners.

"Today, as you set up for workshop, you will see that I have designated rug spots for everyone in our meeting area. You'll see a piece of tape with your name on it in one of the squares on our rug. You'll also see that next to your name is the number 1 or 2, and that the person sitting next to you has the *other* number. That person will be your writing partner. Let's set up for writing workshop. Table monitors, get your caddies! Second-graders, get your notepads! Meet me at the rug."

Tell about one child who used his notepad the evening before to record a tiny detail. Remind children that writers not only *write* but also *live* with details.

"Last year, you wrote Small Moment stories, filled with details, across many pages. Now you are searching, once again, for tiny topics to tell about your lives. Yesterday, we read *Owl Moon*, and some of you said Jane probably jotted 'owling in the morning' in her Tiny Topics notepad before she wrote this story. Will you each take out your notepad and show your writing partner what ideas you have been collecting for future writing projects?" I let the kids quickly share some of their work.

"I forgot to jot down ideas at home," Rocio said, with a questioning tone in her voice, as if to ask, "What should I do?"

"Well, now is always a good time!" I said, then added, "If you are getting an idea just by listening to your partner, jot it down! That's why you carry your notepads." After a minute of sharing, I brought the class back together. "Writers, you are brimming with story ideas! Now what will you do with all these? Hmm, . . . You will turn them into stories!"

❖ **Name the teaching point.**

"Today, writers, I want to teach you how to develop a tiny topic like 'sparkling buildings' into a whole story. Remember, writers don't just think up a topic and then suddenly 'poof,' there is a story. Writers plan and let their stories grow by trying things out and thinking as they write."

You will want to decide on some routines and structures that will give your workshop an efficient flow. Many teachers find it helpful for students to have regular rug spots. This way, rather than negotiating over the place where they will sit each day, students give their full attention to the day's lesson. You may also want to designate numbers or letters to help students decide who will go first in their turn-and-talks. This scaffold is useful if students have a hard time taking turns or just remembering who went first the last time. It also helps to ensure more equity in the conversations.

Think of Tiny Topic notepads as the training wheels for notebooks. They are a place to collect ideas and then, later, to mine for new writing projects. Encourage your students to carry these notepads with them everywhere they go, and to jot ideas in them all the time. This helps your students "try on" the kind of work that grown-up writers do, and it conveys the important message that they can live as writers always, even when they aren't writing.

TEACHING

Tell students that tiny topics don't become stories right away. Instead, writers rehearse how a story will go, planning each part.

"When Jane Yolen wrote *Owl Moon*, she may have gotten the idea for the book from a note she'd written like 'owling at night.' But her story didn't just barge right out. It *grew* in Jane's mind. It went through a lot of rehearsals. Jane might have done a few things to help her plan. Maybe she told the whole story to herself, across her fingers, until it seemed right. Maybe she sketched out how her whole story was going to go and then started writing down the page. You all remember how to do those things from first grade, right? To move more quickly to her draft, Jane might have even written a couple of key words for each part of her story and *then* planned the beginning, middle, and end of *each part*. Her story is *long*!

"Writers, you have some decisions to make. You could practice telling your story across your fingers or you could write key words. Either way, though, you will need to plan!

Demonstrate how you plan a story by telling it across your fingers and by jotting a few key words on each page.

"See, like you, I already wrote some tiny topics in my notepad." I held up a page of my tiny spiral for the children to see. I read, "sparkling buildings." "Watch what I do with the tiny topic I wrote in my notepad so that you can do it, too. Notice how I plan my story and pay attention to the steps I take so you can take them, too!

"Before I write my story, it helps if I tell it to myself. So I am going to do that across my fingers, just like all of you did in first grade. I'm also going to turn to the pages and write a couple of key words to hold onto the parts of my story. I'll write the beginning, middle, and end of each part, down the page. Watch me."

"I have to think what the whole story will be. Hmm. . . . " I held out a clenched hand and began to tell my story. "The rain stopped and I was on a cross-town bus. It was crowded." I uncurled one finger to show that was the first part. I jotted a few key words at the top of the first page of my booklet, then continued telling the story. "Finally we came to my stop. Everyone rushed to the door. I felt crushed." Up went my second finger and again, I jotted a few words, this time on the top of the second page.

I paused as if thinking, and opened my third finger. "We slowly made our way out the door. Suddenly I realized there was a gigantic puddle between the bus and the curb. What was I going to do? I forgot my rain boots! So I decided to jump!"

As I showed children my fourth finger, I whispered, "My story is coming to an end!" Then, I continued, "I jumped with all my might, but I landed right in the center of the puddle. *Splash*! Water flew everywhere!" All the kids laughed.

I held out my last finger. "I jumped up on the curb as quickly as I could. I looked like a drowned rat. I was so upset! But then I looked up and saw those sparkling buildings and felt so much happier!" The kids applauded.

Of course, it's doubtful that Jane told this story across her fingers, but it helps to suggest she may have done something like that! Whether children tell their stories across their fingers or by writing key words at the top of each page in their booklets, saying what they might write, the big lesson is that writers rehearse for writing. They plan.

Here I don't just explain that I first wrote a topic, then wrote a story. Instead, I reenact the process, starting with the words "Watch me." Reenacting (or dramatizing) gives children a demonstration. Demonstrations are vastly more effective than explanations.

Debrief. Recount what you did to plan each page of your story.

"Thank you, writers, but that is just the first step—figuring out how my story goes. Look what I did as I was telling my story." I held up my five-page booklet. Each page had a couple of words jotted at the top. "See, I jotted a couple of words at the top of each page to remember what each part of my story is about. This page is about sitting on the cross-town bus—it says 'Sit on the bus.' (See Figure 3–1.) This page is about getting off and feeling crushed. It says, 'My stop. Crushed.' Each page has the plan of what I am going to write."

Demonstrate writing the beginning, middle, and end of the first page of your story. Then recount all the steps of today's teaching.

Now I'm ready to write the beginning, middle, and end of each page. I'll do the first page right now."

> The rain had just stopped. I was sitting on the cross-town bus, staring out the window, watch-
> ing the sky turn pale blue. I saw people open their jackets. I saw puddles misting in the sun.
> Suddenly I looked up and all around me the buildings were sparkling.

"See how I took a tiny topic and got ready to write? I did three things. First, I thought about how my story was going to go by telling it across my fingers. Then, I jotted a few words across the pages to remember what I wanted to write. Then, I started thinking about the beginning, middle, and end of my first page and got to writing!"

ACTIVE ENGAGEMENT

Ask the class to take an idea from their notepads and grow it into a story, telling the story to a partner.

"Let's try this, right here, right now. Look in your notepad for a story idea that you have filed away. If you don't have one, jot one now quickly. How will your story go? Take out your hand and, just to yourself, start to tell it across your fingers. What did you do or hear or notice first?" I took out my fingers and pretended to tell another story, mumbling under my breath.

"Now, pick up your booklet. Partner 1, tell Partner 2 what key words you might jot down on each page to remember what to write."

LINK

Remind children how Jane Yolen might have gotten the idea for her story, emphasizing that they can do the same—they can find and record small moments.

"Tiny topics are in your lives everywhere! When you go from a tiny topic to a story, remember to give your story time to grow. As you plan your stories, remember, you can do the things you learned last year, but you can also try something new, like jotting down words and planning the beginning, middle, and end of each page."

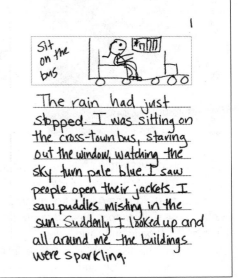

FIG. 3–1   A couple of words jotted at the top of the page reminds writers what each part of the story is about.

Here, I have set children up to try the very thing I described. There are no machinations—children can simply turn to their partner and start. It isn't necessary for children to report back. The point is to give them a minute to try something.

Notice I use a metaphor to describe the writing process. I may want to convene my English language learners and be more explicit about what, "Give your story time to grow means."

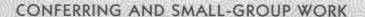

Scaffolding Students to Rehearse Their Writing

A S YOU CONFER TODAY, you're bound to encounter some predictable problems. If you have a group of children whose pieces tend to be disconnected, or told almost as a list, with no clear sense of story, rehearsal will be all the more important. Gather these children together and teach them that they can rehearse their stories by touching each page and saying aloud the words they'll write. You might select one child's story to highlight as an example. Share the child's story with the group, then restate the first page, using more story-like language. If the child says, "I go skating in the park," you might say, "Aha, 'One day, I went skating in the park.'" Then turn to the child and ask, "When, exactly, did you go skating?" After learning the time, show the group how to combine the time and the action. Say, "So Alex might begin his story, '*Yesterday afternoon*, I went skating in the park.' Do you see how now the story has a time and a place?"

Sometimes the feeling of disconnection in a piece of writing comes from sentences that read as stand-alone lines. Imagine Alex's story about skating continues in this way: "I fell down. My knee was bloody. It hurt." Although the parts are told chronologically, they don't yet have a story feel. Here you might show Alex and the rest of the group how to connect the different parts of the story by dressing up the words around them: "*Suddenly*, I fell down. *I looked at* my knee *and saw that it* was bloody. *Ouch! It hurt*." Kids will enjoy watching you add a little drama to their writing, and you, meanwhile, can use this to teach. You won't say, "Look, I added a transition word here, and a conjunction there" (unless you want to turn this into a small-group session on connecting words). Instead, place the emphasis on storytelling in ways that connect all the parts on a page—on writing a story that flows and holds together.

Meanwhile, you will want to also give attention to your more advanced writers as they rehearse and plan. These children may write lively pieces that are sequentially told, with a clear beginning, middle, and end. They may write at some length, elaborating with detail. Often their problem is the opposite of children who write list-like sentences. These children write stories that have an almost breathless, run-on quality. These children also benefit from planning, but their next step may be to give shape to

MID-WORKSHOP TEACHING
Writers Grow Each Page of Their Stories

"Writers, can I stop you for a moment? Listen to what Gresha just did. She had written, 'doing Sara's hair,' in her Tiny Topics notepad to remind her how she does her little sister's hair in the mornings. But she didn't just write that story straight away. Instead, she remembered that Jane Yolen lets her idea *grow in her mind* before she starts writing.

"Listen to how Gresha told *her* story. Instead of just writing on the first page, 'I did my sister's hair,' she starts her story, 'Sara stood on the stool by the mirror. Her hair had knots in it. I brushed and brushed to get the knots out. It was hard to do.' Don't you love how you can hear the beginning, middle, and end of just that very first part of her story? Listen to it again. 'Sara stood on the stool by the mirror. Her hair had knots in it.' That is the beginning. Now listen to the middle. 'I brushed the knots. It was hard to do.' Now listen to the end of the page. 'Sara started to cry.'

"Wow, Gresha, this is only the first page! Writers, do you see how Gresha has told us all about the first part of her story? It's long and detailed, isn't it? She told the beginning of what happened—*and* the middle—*and* the end! Gresha, what happens next?"

"I wiped my sister's tears."

"That's the next page? Beautiful! One page about wiping your sister's tears! I can already imagine it, can't you, second-graders? I'm picturing Gresha getting up, grabbing a tissue, handing it to her sister, or maybe even wiping her sister's face gently herself."

"I also put barrettes in Sara's hair," Gresha offered.

"Does that go on this page?" I turned the page and looked at Gresha. She nodded.

"Writers, will you look at the page you are on, or turn back to the beginning of your book, and think about the beginning, middle, and end of how your page goes? Then share it with your neighbor so that you can be sure you are doing what Gresha is doing—really pushing your story down the page, not just across!

"Okay, back to writing, second-graders. Try and fill up your lines. If you need to use a flap, to extend the page further, there are flaps and staplers in your writing caddies in the center of your table. There are always extra booklets, pages, and flaps in our writing center as well. When you need to, don't forget to get the materials that you need."

As Students Continue Working . . .

"While you've been writing, Kenzy just lost her tooth. She is in the middle of another story, but she didn't want to forget about the tooth, so she jotted it in her Tiny Topics notepad. Some of the rest of you may find that things happen to you, or come to your mind, as you're writing—and I know you'll use your Tiny Topics notepad to hold these ideas for later."

what's already on the page—rather than add to it. Suggest that they read their writing out loud to see how it sounds—and which parts are especially full of details, and which ones a little more sparse. Then they can return to their writing and think about whether they've elaborated in ways that work best to showcase their story.

Consider, for example, Rocio's piece, "Come Out Snail!" (see Figure 3–2). Notice how Rocio has made a plan for what to write by jotting a couple words at the top of each page, along with a quick sketch. The strategy has clearly worked for her as each page does, in fact, follow her plan.

Notice, too, that the words and sketches have helped Rocio write with focus; this is a Small Moment story.

Look at the piece again. Do all the parts feel equal? In fact, some parts are more elaborated upon than others. Certainly, you won't expect children to elaborate in equal amounts on each part of a story, but for advanced writers like Rocio, a natural next step might be to ask themselves whether they have elaborated in ways that show the reader what most matters about this story. Rocio might look at her story's beginning, middle, and end, and ask, "Do I need to add details to any of these parts to make them jump out more?" and "Do I need to delete some of the details that aren't that important?" She might notice, for example, that the color of the snail's shell doesn't have anything to do with the happenings with the snail, but the fact that kids were nervous to touch it does. Maybe she wants to tell about what the shell feels like, instead. She might decide to build up her first two pages to show how nervous the kids were as they got ready to hold and touch the snail. Rocio might also discover that the part in which the snail comes out is well elaborated, but it reads more as a summary than a story. This is where rehearsal is key. If Rocio were to practice reading aloud her story, she would hear the places where it feels more like telling, and less like a story.

Of course, your children will have written pieces on topics other than a snail in a classroom, but the suggestions to Rocio about her story are transferable to any more-advanced writer. Thinking about which details bring out meaning, and checking to be sure a piece is elaborated across the pages rather than in just one part are tips that will apply to any child who is ready to take his or her story to the next level.

(continues)

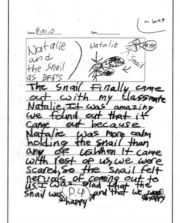

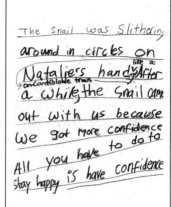

It was first grade, the twins in my class brought their pet snail. The color shell was beige and white. It was so cool!

The twins took out the snail, and started passing the snail around in our hands.

The snail would not get out of its glimmering shell. Some people got nervous, because they thought it was injured, or dead, or just scared of us.

The snail finally came out with my classmate Natalie. It was amazing. We found out that it came out because Natalie was more calm holding the snail than any of us. When it came with the rest of us, we were scared. So, the snail felt nervous coming out to us. I was glad that the snail was happy and that we were happy.

The snail was slithering around in circles on Natalie's hand like an uncontrollable train. After a while, the snail came out with us because we got more confidence. All you have to do to stay happy is have confidence.

FIG. 3–2 Rocio's "Come Out Snail!"

Reading Like Writers

Remind writers of ways to prepare for the writing workshop.

"Writers, before you come over to the meeting area, decide whether your piece of writing is 'finished for now' or whether you are still working on it—whether it's 'a work in progress.' If a piece is 'finished for now,' place it on the red-dot side of your folder. If it is 'still in progress,' place it on the green-dot side. When you have decided, place your folders in the caddy at your tables and join me in the meeting area—quickly and . . . " "Quietly!" the class shouted.

"Can you say that *quietly*? Let's try it again! Quickly and . . . " "Quietly," the class whispered this time.

Channel children to notice and name important parts of the mentor text during a read-aloud.

"Writers, I once read advice that Jane Yolen offered to young writers like yourselves. Do you know what her first suggestion was? 'Read, read, read! You must read every day, and try to read a wide range of books' (janeyolen.com). So I thought, in our share, let's do just that. Let's read *Owl Moon* and think about the different parts of Jane's story! Then let's pick out which ones feel the most important and why we think so. Ready? Let's read."

Turn children's Tiny Topics notepads into necklaces they can wear everywhere they go, gathering ideas for writing.

"Earlier, some of you were asking if you could carry your Tiny Topics notepads around with you at lunch and on the playground to write down more tiny details that you don't want to forget. That's a good idea. I'll help you turn your notepads into necklaces so you can carry them everywhere." I quickly connected students' notepads to lanyards they could wear around their necks.

"Can I take home a booklet as well?" Elizabeth asked.

"Yes, of course. Writers, before you go home today, remember to pack your notepads. If you want to take a booklet or two home, like Elizabeth, to write your stories down tonight, you'll have time this afternoon to collect the things you need."

New materials are a major source of motivation for little children, so parse the new materials out bit by bit when the time is right. The necklaces make the notepads more portable so it's perfect to bring this adaptation now. You could also use yarn to create notepad necklaces.

Writing with Detail
Magnifying a Small Moment

IN THIS SESSION, you'll teach students that writers zoom in on a small moment in their stories, magnifying it with details so that their readers can take it in with all their senses.

GETTING READY

✔ One concrete object (we use seashells) for each partnership to study closely (see Connection)

✔ One set of magnifying glasses, for each partnership or small group to share (see Connection)

✔ *Owl Moon*, by Jane Yolen, or another mentor text to study zooming in on a small moment (see Teaching)

✔ Your own Small Moment story, the one you started in Session 3 (see Teaching)

✔ Student writing folders (see Active Engagement)

✔ "Writers Use Descriptive Details So Readers Can Envision the Story" chart (see Active Engagement)

✔ Tools for revision, including revision strips and flaps, scissors, tape, and staplers (see Link)

✔ Student writing folders, Post-its, and pens (see Share)

✔ One or two student examples of revision (see Share)

L AST YEAR, STUDENTS LEARNED how to select a small moment (seed) topic rather than a much larger (watermelon) topic. Today, you will give them a new metaphor to describe the work not of choosing an idea, but of stretching out a small moment with detail. You'll suggest that children "magnify" their small moments, noticing and recording what they see. This provides a concrete image of the work you hope children do, and it also links narrative writing to the work children have done in the content areas. We suggest you bring in as many magnifying glasses as you can so that children can first examine seashells (or another object of your choice), and then share the details they notice. By setting children up to think across various contexts, applying what they learn in one to the other, you set them up to engage in the kind of strategic, high-level cognitive work that Norman Webb describes as Level 4 in his Depth of Knowledge (DOK).

Although the teaching in this session is about seeing, you won't stop there. You'll tell children that writers use all of their senses to write. They notice and record not only what they see, but also what they hear, feel, smell, and taste to describe a moment in detail. They pay close attention to everything about the small moment they are trying to describe so that their readers can experience that moment as if they, too, were there. This is important work. Few things are as essential to good writing as writing "small" about something big. When children write about their lives with precise details, not generalities, when they record the exact sensory elements of that moment, they create lush, powerful narratives.

Today's session sets the stage for the craft work you will do in Bend III. It also reinforces a big theme of the unit—living like a writer. Your hope is that children will transfer this close study of the world not only to other writing units of study, but to the way they live outside of your room and outside of school.

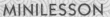

Writing with Detail
Magnifying a Small Moment

CONNECTION

Introduce the concrete object children will study closely—seashells, flowers, or something else with details—and then give one to each set of partners.

"Writers, give me a thumbs up if you've ever been to the beach." A flurry of thumbs went up. "Oh wow, lots of you have visited the beach! Thumbs up again if you collected shells when you were at the beach." Again, thumbs flew up. "Look at all the shell collectors we have in this room! Guess what, writers? I went to the beach this summer, and I collected shells, too. Look—I brought in some of my favorites. I'm going to pass these around. Partner 1, when you have a shell, put it between you and Partner 2. You two will share the shell in just a second."

Teachers, you may need to alter this example to one that will ring true for your class. If you do not live close to the beach, perhaps you'll ask kids whether they have ever picked flowers in a park or a field (and then, of course, you'll need to bring in flowers they can study).

Set children up to make close observations of their objects, zooming in on the details with the help of a magnifying glass.

Once each partnership had a shell I said, "Writers, remember last year when we studied worms in science? You looked at those really closely to describe what you noticed. You looked through magnifying glasses and saw lines on the worms' bodies, and watched how the worms moved. Right now, you are going to look *that* closely at your shells. I'm going to give each partnership a magnifying glass that will help you zoom in on the details of your shell. Pick up your shells and look closely at them. Talk to your partner about the things you notice."

If you don't have magnifying glasses, you can ask children to pretend they have them, and to look really, really closely, aiming to see details.

As children talked, I listened in, taking note of their observations. Then I reconvened the class.

Share some childrens' observations, pointing out the kinds of details they noticed.

"Writers, I want to share some of the things I heard you say just now. Lots of you described the colors of your shell. You said things like, 'It's pink and white' or 'It's light brown.' Some of you noticed the markings on your shell—lines and dots, squiggles and swirls. And some of you described the shapes of your shells—I heard words like *round*, *oval*, *fan-shaped*, *cones*. Great noticing, writers. You really saw lots of detail in your shells. One of my favorite authors, Kate DiCamillo, once said, 'Writing is seeing. It is paying attention.'"

❖ **Name the teaching point.**

"Writers, that kind of seeing, paying attention, is at the heart of living a writerly life. Today, I want to teach you that when writers want to zoom in on a small moment, to capture it so that readers see it as they do, they magnify it, by writing with lots of details."

TEACHING

Study one page of the mentor text, noticing how the author zooms in on a small moment to write with detail.

"Let me show you what I mean. I'm going to turn to a page in *Owl Moon*. I could pick any page to model this, so I'll just pick one randomly." I flipped open the book to the third page. "As I read, pay attention to the details Jane Yolen includes to describe this moment."

> *We reached the line*
> *of pine trees,*
> *black and pointy*
> *against the sky,*
> *and Pa held up his hand.*
> *I stopped right where I was*
> *and waited.*
> *He looked up,*
> *as if searching the stars,*
> *as if reading a map up there.*
> *The moon made his face*
> *into a silver mask.*
> *Then he called:*
> *"Whoo-whoo-who-who-who-whoooooooo,"*
> *the sound of a Great Horned Owl.*
> *"Whoo-whoo-who-who-who-whoooooooo."*

"Wow, I have goose bumps. The way Jane has written this, it's as if she held up a magnifying glass to this moment, just like each of you did with your shells just now. She could have just written, 'We reached the trees. Pa made an owl noise,' but that wouldn't have had nearly the same effect. So instead, she stretched out this moment with lots of tiny details that allow us to see the scene just as she imagined it.

"The first thing I notice is how Jane describes the pine trees as 'black and pointy against the sky.' It's like I'm seeing those trees through a magnifying glass—so tall they touch the sky!

"What else do I see? Hmm, . . . Oh! This part about how Pa 'looked up, as if searching the stars, as if reading a map up there.' Again, it's like Jane Yolen has magnified the moment for us. I can picture how intently Pa is studying the sky, can you?

Here, you model for children how to envision a moment, step by step, and invite them to notice with you how Jane Yolen uses details to draw the reader in. The goal is that children feel the power of descriptive writing—how it can put a reader right into the world of a story.

"I'll stop there. I'm sure we'll be looking at this part again sometime soon because there is so much in it to notice. But right now, it's enough to study how Jane magnifies the details she notices so that her reader can see them, too."

Demonstrate how to write like the mentor author, zooming in on your own Small Moment story and magnifying it with lots of details.

"So writers, if I were to do like Jane does and like what we as scientists do, I could try to write my own small moment by looking at it through an imaginary magnifying glass. Let me do that and think about what I might add. Here's the second page of my piece about riding the bus." I put my second page up on the white board (see Figure 4–1).

Finally we came to my stop. Everyone rushed to the door. I felt crushed.

"Hmm, . . . No details here yet. So let's see. If I want my readers to see exactly what I saw, as if they're looking through a magnifying glass at this little scene, what could I add? Well, I might include what I saw. I remember lots of people all around me. There was a tall man wearing headphones, and a couple of teenage girls, whose linked arms blocked my path. It was hard to squeeze through. If I add those details, my page might go like this:

Finally we came to my stop. Everyone rushed to the door. A tall man, wearing headphones, swayed his body as he barged ahead of me. Two teenage girls, arms linked, blocked my path, making a barricade. I felt crushed.

"Is that clearer, writers? Can you see what happened on the bus with those new details added?" The kids nodded.

Notice that I have included a word that many second-graders may not know: barricade. This is intentional. It introduces children to new vocabulary, and allows me to scaffold them as they learn. As I talk about the scene on the bus I use other words children will know—blocked my path—to introduce what barricade means.

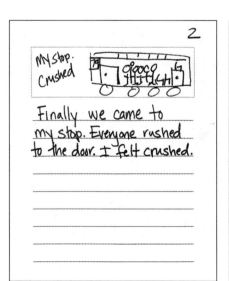

FIG. 4–1   First draft of page 2   Revised draft of page 2

ACTIVE ENGAGEMENT

Challenge writers to zoom in on a small moment in their own stories, writing with detail. Offer suggestions as they work.

"Writers, it's your turn to try this with your own writing. Open up your folders and take out the story you wrote yesterday." I gave them a second to do this. "Find a part of your story that's a little bare right now, that could use magnifying for your reader." After a moment, I said, "Now, turn to your partner and help each other 'hold magnifying glasses'"—I made quotation marks with my fingers—"to your writing."

I coached into partnerships, "Help your partner think of the details that will help a reader picture what is there and what is happening."

LINK

Send students off to write, and encourage them to add detail to their stories. Tuck in reminders of how to add on to their writing, and demonstrate one way.

"It may seem easy at first to add a detail here or there. But to add in details the way that writers like Jane Yolen do is hard work. It will take time and certainly a lot of practice! You can work on this as you write today. Some of you might be starting new stories, and some of you might be adding into ones that you have finished.

"Rocio was worried that she had no more space to add details. Remember, though, in first grade how in your writing center you had strips, flaps, and Post-its to add details *anywhere* in your writing? We have those, too. They are in your writing caddies and in the writing center if you run out. You can stick them *anywhere* on the page. You can line one up exactly with the line where you want to add on, or you can write the number 1 in the space where you want to add some writing and a number 1 on your Post-it, so that you know where the writing goes. Let me show you." I gave a quick demo to show them what this would look like in my writing.

"I hope you will take this challenge, and try to *magnify* your stories so that your readers will feel like they are right there—beside you. I'll be on the lookout for the ways in which you do this. At the end of writing workshop, you'll have a chance to share how you used details to tell your small moments in *big* ways."

WRITERS Use Descriptive Details So READERS Can Envision the Story

WRITERS		READERS
...weave setting details throughout the story.		...envision the scene the character is in by paying attention to setting clues.
...use strong action words to show exactly what the character is doing.	raced bolted / leaps sprung	...envision what the characters are doing by paying attention to their specific behaviors.
...include dialogue and dialogue tags to show exactly what the character says and how he/she says it.	shouted / whispered	...notice what the character says and envision how he/she says it by paying attention to dialogue and dialogue tags.

Dramatizing Action to Help Students Write with Detail

YOU WILL FIND THAT many of your conferences today focus on writing with detail. Be sure, as you work with kids, that you don't just tell them to add detail, but instead help them to do so. That is, give your students demonstrations rather than directions. This is especially important because if you don't teach otherwise, children will flesh out a barebones story with insignificant details that do little for the story—or the reader. A story that once read, "Today my school bus almost crashed into a car," may now read "Today my big, yellow school bus almost crashed into a big, green car."

I watched as Heather reread her six-page booklet (Figure 4–2) and added the detail about Chelsea Piers onto her first page. "What a lucky time for you—making a strike!" I said. "In all my life, I have never made a strike." I asked her a few questions about her process and learned that she'd made a movie in her mind before writing. The results were clear—in one portion of her story.

"When you do something that works," I taught her, "try to do it on many pages. And, when you do so, go beyond making a movie in your mind of what happened. Reenact what happened. Let's try this together. Is there a part in your story where you envision even more?"

Heather reread the page and said, "I was worried that the pins wouldn't go down."

"Hmm . . . I know that feeling, but what about readers who've never bowled? Think you can tell exactly what happened, in detail, so that they can see and feel your worry?" Heather nodded. I pointed to the sentence that said, 'I held the ball.' Try to remember exactly what you were doing and thinking. Pretend you are at the bowling alley. Show me what you did, and say what you thought."

Heather clambered to her feet and assumed bowling position. "See, I held the ball in my hands," she said and held an imaginary ball. As I recorded what Heather said, I prompted, "What did you think?"

MID-WORKSHOP TEACHING
Writers Use All Their Senses to Add Details to Their Stories

"One, two, three, all eyes on me!" I called out.

"One, two, eyes on you!" the children called back.

"Now that I have your attention, I want to teach you one more thing about writing with details. Writers don't just talk about what they *see*. They use all their senses when they describe scenes. Take our shells, for example. We could put them up to our ears and describe the sounds we hear. We could say, 'It's like the ocean in there!' and 'There's a whoosh whoosh sound.' Or we could notice how the shells feel. We could say, 'The shells are smooth and silky.'

"Jane does the same thing in her story, right? She writes the sounds of the owl. 'Whoo-whoo-who-who-who-whooooooo!' You all can try that, too. You can add in details that are not just about what you *see*, but about what you *hear*, what you *feel*, or even what you *smell* or *taste*—if that's important to your story! Look back in your book and think about the details that you are adding—can you try and use all your senses as you write to help you zoom in on your moment? Try it right now in your story. If you think you can, don't waste a minute—just add it in!"

"I thought it would go in the gutters."

"Keep going. Act out what you did next," I said.

"I let the ball go," Heather said, reenacting in slow motion the way she released the ball.

(continues)

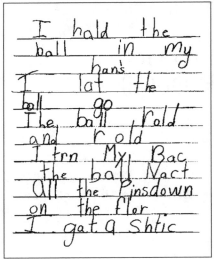

Once at my birthday party I made a strike. My birthday party was at Chelsea Piers.

I held the ball in my hands. I let the ball go. The ball rolled and rolled. I turned my back. The ball knocked all the pins down on the floor. "I got a strike."

FIG. 4–2   Heather writes with tiny actions after dramatizing the part out loud.

"Say exactly what you did."

"My arm went down and my, my waist went down," she said, as she reenacted the position bowlers take as they release the ball. "Then I looked away 'cause I didn't want to see it," she said.

"And then?" I prompted.

"Then I saw it and I said, 'I got a strike! I got a strike!'" Heather said, reenacting how she jumped for glee.

"Heather, I recorded what you said. Will you reread your writing and ask yourself, 'Is there anything I should add on that shows the exact story of what happened when I went bowling?'" I opened her book to the page we'd discussed at some length.

I reread my transcript of what she'd described. Soon Heather had added to her page.

Wrapping up the conference, I reminded Heather of the steps that we followed to show more, and reiterated that often just using her body would help her to "magnify the details." In this way, I emphasized the strategy she could use on another day and with a different piece.

Turning to Classmates as Mentors

Highlight the work of two students who used details to zoom in on small moments.

"One two three, all eyes on me." The students all stopped what they were doing immediately this time. "Remember what you say back? One . . . ," I prompted. They chimed in, "One two, all eyes on you!"

"Will you bring over your writing, a Post-it from your caddy, and a pen? Let's gather in the meeting area. Quickly and quietly, find your rug spot!" As children took their places, I gave every partnership a copy of writing done by one of their classmates.

"Writers, I'm givng you a copy of a piece of writing that Kenzy did. We'll study this closely, almost as if we are studying it through a magnifying lens."

I pointed to an enlarged copy of Kenzy's draft and said, "Listen to Kenzy's first version of her story beginning." (See Figure 4–3.)

> One summer morning I was in my country Egypt and at my grandma's house. Today I was going to see the pyramids so I got dressed super quickly and me and my mom and my sister went to the car.

"After she wrote this, she decided to magnify the details, to show much more," I said. "As I read Kenzy's second draft, follow along on your copy, noticing and underlining ways she added details to help you imagine you are in Egypt with her."

> One summer morning I was in my country Egypt and at my grandma's house. It was super hot. My grandma's house has a balcony. Today I was going to see the pyramids. "Inty rayha al pyramids," said my grandma. So I got dressed super quickly. "Hurry up," I said, and me and my mom and my sister went to the car. In the car I heard the air conditioner beeping. My family was so nice to let me go see the pyramids in the summer.

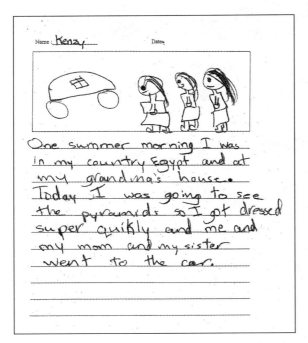

FIG. 4–3 Page one of Kenzy's draft has sparse details.

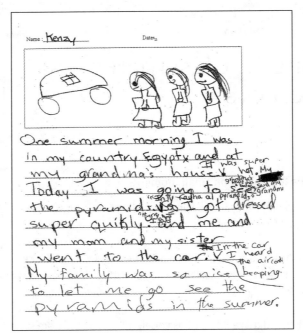

Page one of Kenzy's revised draft includes dialogue in Arabic and other small details that allow the reader to envision the story.

"Turn and talk about the details Kenzy added," I said.

I listened as April asked her partner about the words Kenzy's grandmother used. "It's Arabic," Kenzy explained.

"You are right. She included dialogue, what people said," I said, naming the craft move. "She used her first language, Arabic. That really helps us imagine life in her grandma's house in Egypt, doesn't it? What a wise decision to write in both languages!"

I convened the class, noting to them all, "April realized that Kenzy didn't just tell us what people said, she used their language to show exactly what and how they said it!" I let the class name a few more things.

Debrief. Name the big work of the day and rally students to set goals for tomorrow's workshop.

"Wow, writers! You noticed so many things! Right now, jot on a Post-it something you want to try tomorrow. I have extra Post-it notes if you want to write two or three things." "Put the Post-its on the part of your writing where you'll do this work."

"Writers, now we have a plan for tomorrow! Put your writing on the 'In Progress' side of your folder. Then put your folder away. Table monitors, put your writing caddies back in the writing center. Ready, set, everyone—off you go to do your jobs!"

Revising with the Masters
Crafting Powerful Endings

ear Teachers,

On the very first day of this unit, you read aloud the opening lines of two whole-class mentor texts. You read them with care, before asking children to think about what may have prompted Angela Johnson to write about "the leaving morning" and Jane Yolen about one night of "owling." There's a reason you read these opening lines aloud. You wanted your students to feel the rhythm and craft these master writers bring to their beginnings. Through these masters, your students learned that beginnings matter. Beginnings establish the tone and mood of a book. They set the stage for what's to come. And above all, they invite the reader in.

Today's session echoes what you did on Day One, but this time you'll shine a spotlight on endings, drawing again on the masters to highlight the type of work students can emulate. You'll teach children that just as beginnings lure the reader in, endings bring the reader home. A good ending, the right ending, carves out a little place in our minds and hearts. It stays with us long after we've put the book down. All too often children rush through their endings, eager to begin a new project. Today's session teaches them to slow down. It teaches them that crafting a powerful ending is an essential step in the writing process.

There is another reason to teach a revision session on story endings. Most state standards expect that second-graders can describe the structure of a story, including how the beginning introduces the story and the ending concludes the action. Today's session supports and extends this emphasis on structure. It gives children some concrete ways to think about revising a story ending so that it brings the story full circle.

Today, then, you'll teach children that they can turn to their mentor texts to help them write powerful endings. You'll study a few endings from favorite class stories, noticing and naming what each author is doing that students can try in their own writing. This session, then, is not just about writing endings. It also teaches students that they can turn to mentor texts for inspiration whenever they revise.

Today's session explores more than story endings. It introduces students to large-scale revision. The goal is that students leave today with the understanding that revision requires more than just adding in a bit here and there. It requires looking across a piece of writing, thinking, "What do I need to strengthen?"

MINILESSON

You might begin the minilesson by rereading the beginnings of the two whole-class mentor texts and then reminding children what they noticed about these. Both beginnings describe the setting—the sounds and sights—of the story. They transport the reader into the woods at night to go owling, and up against a window on "the leaving morning." Remind students that story beginnings set the stage for what's to come.

Then you might say, "Writers, story beginnings matter. And so do endings. Today, I want to teach you that professional writers spend lots of time writing and rewriting their endings. You can study these authors to learn how they craft their endings. This will give you ideas for how to bring your own story to a satisfying end."

During the teaching you might pass out copies of the ending lines of both *Owl Moon* and *The Leaving Morning*. Ask children to turn and talk to their partners about what they notice. Then share out some of their observations. They may say that *Owl Moon* begins with a journey into the woods and ends with a return home. They may notice that the book ends with the words of the title, *owl moon*, or that the author conveys a message at the end about having hope (and perhaps, if your children are particularly attuned to comparisons by now, that hope is likened to an owl).

Children may remark that Angela Johnson begins and ends *The Leaving Morning* with the little boy making lips on the window. They will probably notice that this book also ends with the words of its title, *the leaving morning*. Perhaps your more advanced students will realize that whereas *Owl Moon* begins with an adventure and ends with a return home, *The Leaving Morning* ends with a good-bye and the start of a new adventure—taking the characters away from home.

You might begin to name and make a temporary chart about what makes for a "good ending." Good endings echo the beginning, leave the reader with something to think about, bring the story full circle, solve a problem, or bring out the meaning of the story. Next, you could model how to revise one of your own story endings by trying some of these moves. Rather than incorporating all things into a single ending, try out different things in a string of endings—so that children see that authors craft several endings before deciding on one that fits. Perhaps first you'll create an echo between your story beginning and ending (with the language or the imagery). Next, you might write an ending that gives the reader something to think about—a realization or a reflection. Finally, you might write an ending that resolves the issue or puts something to rest. Each ending you write should bring your narrative to a natural conclusion, so that children have models of how to do the same.

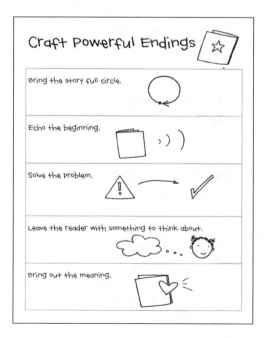

Craft Powerful Endings

Bring the story full circle.

Echo the beginning.

Solve the problem.

Leave the reader with something to think about.

Bring out the meaning.

Above all, you'll want children to understand that an ending completes a story's action. Show children how to study their mentors for ideas to bring their story's action to a close. It will be challenging for children to duplicate the beautiful language and craft exemplified by writers like Jane and Angela, so be prepared to welcome their approximations.

For the active engagement, children could work in partnerships to talk through some possible ways their endings might go. Remind them to use the class chart on endings and their mentor texts for ideas. They can jot ideas on Post-it notes that they then affix to the story they are currently writing, or have recently written. Rather than jumping from one story to another, encourage them to stick with a single story that is particularly meaningful to them. Often, we encourage children to think and write quickly during workshop. Today, you'll want them to linger a bit, to take time creating lasting images, trying out new things in their writing, carefully choosing words—and to feel the pleasure of crafting an ending that feels just right.

As you send children off to write, remind them of the many things they've learned from the masters to make writing more powerful. Then reiterate that crafting a new ending is one move they may want to try today—or any day—as they prepare for the celebration. Say, "Writers, all around you are examples of carefully crafted endings," as you point to the bookshelves and the writing caddies. "You might want to read some of these for inspiration." Remind them that just as they have studied endings, they can study *any* part of a mentor text to help them revise their writing, trying it out a few different ways. As children go off to write, read aloud the endings of *Owl Moon* and *The Leaving Morning*.

CONFERRING AND SMALL-GROUP WORK

In *Opening Minds* (2012) and *Choice Words* (2004), Peter Johnston reminds us how important it is to convey to students that writing well is hard work—and that working hard on projects that matter is a privilege. It isn't just second graders who look at beautiful literature and imagine it flew directly out of a writer's imagination and onto the page. Adults, too, often bear that impression. That's because when writing is done well, it has an effortless feel. The reality, though, is that more often than not, it takes rounds and rounds of revisions to craft something just right.

In your conferences and small groups, then, be sure you recognize the effort and hard work students are investing in their writing, and that they understand that this work is of their own making. You may be teaching them strategies to try out in their writing, and the mentor author your class is studying is of course teaching them craft, but each child in the room has authored a collection of narratives that bears that child's voice, stamp, and, yes, effort.

Now it is up to students to determine what their pieces still need and to set goals for themselves. Emphasize that goal-setting of this kind is important. It means deciding what, of all of the many revision moves one can make, will achieve the needed effect to make this piece of writing have a polished, seamless feel. All learners—professional piano players, sports figures, teachers—acknowledge that mastering a skill involves setting personal goals and working hard to achieve them.

As you confer today, you have an important job. Now that you have positioned children to set and reach important revision goals, it is up to you to find out what constitutes this 'kind of revision for each of your learners. Ask children to show you how they are working hard to make their stories even better by pointing to specific revisions they have made, or places in the text they intend to revise.

If your students describe the sorts of changes that can be added by means of a caret, like a single word addition, you'll know you need to steer them toward more substantial revision plans. If the revisions a child indicates are small editing moves that don't actually lift the meaning or the quality of his story, you'll want to give that writer feedback so that he understands how to think and revise as a professional writer does. To do that, you might take these steps:

- Name what the student has done.
- Explain that he is ready to take on more extensive revision, revision that is heftier than a word change—sometimes this means moving around whole sections of text, elaborating in places that are sparse, deleting details that aren't important, and so on.
- Then support the student with a revision strategy that will make a gigantic difference to his particular story. For example, the child might add dialogue and actions to his story to bring the characters to life, or he might tell more about what he noticed all around him to make the setting more vivid.
- Then watch while he gets started, coaching if needed.
- Circle back later to be sure he has learned the strategy well enough that he can use it to revise next time he works on a piece.

MID-WORKSHOP TEACHING

For your mid-workshop teaching, you could teach children that writers don't just make little ticky-tacky revisions, changing a word here, or deleting a line there. They make large-scale revisions, focusing on whole sections of their stories at a time. In addition to endings, writers revise beginnings. They think, "Have I set up my story the way I want it to? Does it set the stage for what's to come? Does it create the mood or feeling I want? Does it hook readers, making them want to read on?" They also revise the most exciting, or sad, or revealing part, making sure to slow down and stretch that part out.

SHARE

Before ending the workshop, you could share-out some of the endings children have crafted (or recrafted) today. Read these aloud and then point out what, exactly, the writers did to good effect—or open this up for discussion, instead inviting responses from the class. Then ask children to talk to a partner about how their endings emulate—or mimic—the endings in their favorite mentor texts. Ask, "What ideas have you taken from the masters to try out in your writing?" Emphasize that they can always turn to mentor texts anytime they are revising their writing, and to work on any part of their piece.

Good luck,
Amanda and Julia

Session 6

Rereading Like Detectives
Making Sure Writing Makes Sense and Sounds Right

A S YOU TEACH CHILDREN how to write with special attention to detail, to meaning, to craft, you will want to devote some of your minilessons also to teaching the conventions of grammar. In their eagerness to exercise their growing writing skills, second-graders tend to write a lot, often at the expense of clarity. You will of course celebrate this zeal and the volume of writing your students produce, but meanwhile, it is important that you arm your children with tools to clarify their writing. They should certainly be in the habit of checking for capitalization, punctuation, and spelling, noticing when something doesn't look or sound right, and then using their knowledge and resources to fix these parts.

In this session, then, you will teach children specific strategies for how to attend to one important grammar convention: punctuation. Specifically, you'll teach them to check that sentences don't run on and on with a series of *and*s. You'll teach them how to reread to determine when a sentence has gone on too long and to then end it with a period before beginning the next one. You can decide whether to teach your class a second convention during the mid-workshop and even a third during the share. Perhaps you'll focus on spelling in one and on capitalization in the other. Or you could see what your particular students discover on their own as they write, and then spotlight these for the whole class.

Notice that today's session builds on prior instruction to look closely. Whereas previously, students received magnifying glasses to drive home the point that writers zoom in on important details, today they'll learn to look closely at their writing just as detectives look closely at clues—to be sure that their writing has correct punctuation.

We selected ending punctuation because our years of research have shown that second-grade students writing at benchmark have a tendency to write endless, breathless sentences. The mid-workshop on commas, though taken from an actual child's discovery, is the perfect add-on to today's teaching because it gives another way to clarify an otherwise muddled sentence. If your particular class of students has these conventions under its belt, you might instead teach a minilesson on paragraphing or on complex sentences,

IN THIS SESSION, you'll teach children that writers reread their writing like detectives, checking the ending punctuation to make sure it makes sense and sounds right to the reader.

GETTING READY

✔ Pages 3 and 4 of the demonstration story you started in Session 3, written on chart paper or to project on an overhead. Page 3 should show many run-on sentences, and Page 4 should have correct end punctuation (see Connection)

✔ Students' writing and pens (see Active Engagement)

✔ Students' writing folders, Post-it notes, and pens (see Share)

✔ Page 4 of your demonstration story, with at least one misspelled word (see Share)

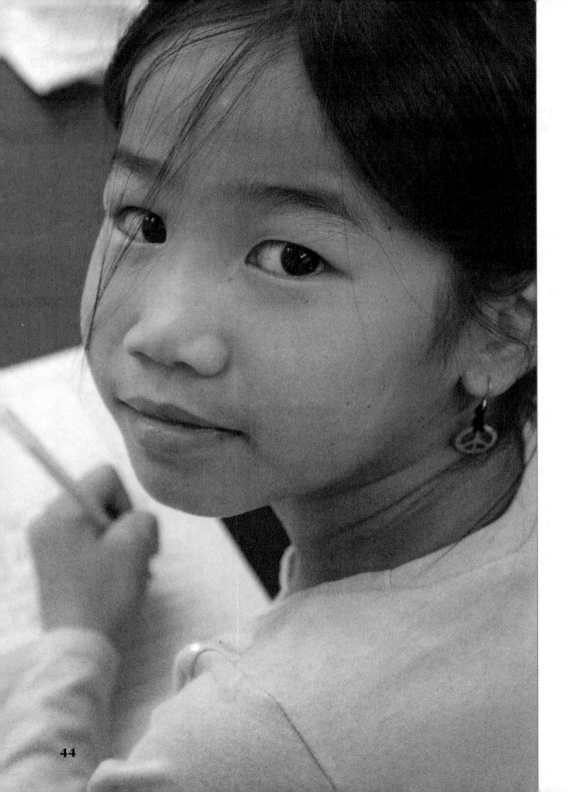

> *"In this session . . . you will teach children specific strategies for how to attend to one important grammar convention: punctuation."*

or on beginning dictionary work. The important thing is that you teach whatever conventions your children most need at this stage in their writing lives (and, of course, you'll also use one-on-one conferences and small-group work to help particular children with the conventions they are struggling to understand), and that you position children to meet world-class standards.

44

Rereading Like Detectives
Making Sure Writing Makes Sense and Sounds Right

CONNECTION

Share with students two pages from your demonstration text—one page with many run-on sentences and one page with correct end punctuation.

"One, two, three, all eyes on me!" I chanted. After the kids made their reponse, I asked them to bring a piece of writing from their writing folder and a pen to the meeting area.

"I have two pages of writing—pages three and four of my story about the sparkling buildings. Will you all be detectives and quickly study my two pages? Specifically, pay attention to my punctuation. Read aloud with me. Are you ready?" I pointed to the two enlarged pages.

By now, this attention-getting device should be old hat for your class.

The doors opened and I quickly pushed to the front of the stairs and then I suddenly saw a gigantic puddle and I didn't know what to do and I forgot my rain boots and I decided to jump over the puddle and I jumped.

The doors opened AND I quickly pushed to the front of the stairs AND then I suddenly saw a gigantic puddle AND I didn't know what to do AND I forgot my rain boots AND I decided to jump over the puddle AND I jumped.

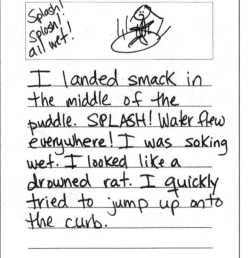

I landed smack in the middle of the puddle. SPLASH! Water flew everywhere! I was soking wet. I looked like a drowned rat. I quickly tried to jump up onto the curb.

I landed smack in the middle of the puddle. SPLASH! Water flew everywhere! I was soking wet. I looked like a drowned rat. I quickly tried to jump up onto the curb.

FIG. 6–1   Pages 3 and 4 of the story about sparkling buildings

Recruit students to turn-and-talk, observing what is different about the two pages. Then share out some of their observations.

"What do you notice about the punctuation on the two pages?" I asked. I listened in to partnerships and jotted down a few things they mentioned to one another. Some kids noticed right away that the third page was filled with *ands* and the fourth page wasn't. I prompted those students to think about which page looked and sounded better—and how to fix the other.

"Let me share what some of your classmates found. Joey and Kareem found that on page 3 there are many *ands* and only one period. They saw that on page 4 there were no *ands* and six punctuation marks. Did anyone else see that? Put your thumb on your knee if you saw that too or if you see it now.

"Great detective work, writers. I want to talk to you today about punctuation because I took your work home and saw lots of great details. But in some pieces I saw *no* punctuation marks. In other pieces, I saw too many *ands*. I know that in first grade you all studied end punctuation to make your writing clear. Sometimes when you are writing quickly—and this happens to me, too—you forget to write with punctuation."

❖ **Name the teaching point.**

"Today, I want to teach you that writers reread to make sure both that their writing says what they want it to say and that it makes sense. They look for end punctuation. To build this writing habit, it can help to stop after each page, reread, and ask, 'Did I use punctuation on this page so that it makes sense?' "

TEACHING

Demonstrate how to reread your own writing, pausing to look for and include end punctuation.

"Watch as I do a punctuation check on my writing. As I reread, I'll consider whether the writing will make sense to my reader. If not, I"ll decide where I need punctuation and what kind of punctuation I need. Watch as I do this, so you can think along with me. If you think I need punctuation, just put your thumb on your hand like this"—I made a motion as if I was stamping something with my thumb.

"Here I go." I began to read. "The doors opened *and* I pushed to the front of the stairs *and* then I suddenly saw . . . " By now kids were stamping their hands with their thumbs. "Yes, I agree with you. I need to slow this part down with some punctuation, so it will make sense to my reader. I could put a period after the word *opened* (The door opened. I pushed to the front . . .) or after *stairs* (. . . to the front of the stairs. I suddenly saw . . .). Either option would work, but if I say I did this *and* I did this *and* I did . . . that's too many *ands*. See, punctuation takes thought! I'm glad I am rereading this." I added a period after *stairs* and reread just that sentence. "Much better!"

Some teachers emphasize that periods tell the reader to pause; others tie the period to meaning. Either way, children won't "get it right" without repeated practice. Sometimes teachers tell us that their children "can't even write with periods" as if this is a simple, elementary thing to do. It's not. Determining where sentences end is a complex matter. It's easier to decide between types of ending marks than it is to know when a sentence ends.

When teaching young children, I find it helps to put myself in their shoes, imagining their experience of doing something. Rereading my writing in order to add end punctuation is easy for me because I find the syntactical units that comprise a text. A child who is just learning this will need to read the text one way and another way before settling on "the right way." Because young children can't usually articulate their processes, it will benefit them to watch and hear me voice mine.

Invite students to read and think alongside you as you demonstrate on the next sentence.

"Now let me see about this next sentence. Read along in your heads with me, and use your thumbs again as stamps! 'And then I suddenly saw a gigantic puddle *and* I didn't know what to do *and*.'" I stopped again, out of breath. "Thanks for stamping your thumbs again. Looks like I have another decision. I have to get rid of some of these *ands*! I"ll get rid of this first one, and the word *then* (see Figure 6–2). It will sound better, 'Suddenly, I . . .' Do you agree?"

The students nodded.

"Thank you, detectives! That was so helpful. I'll continue rereading and fixing up this page! When I am done with this part, I'll reread my whole book for two things: details and punctuation."

ACTIVE ENGAGEMENT

Set students up to fix their stories' punctuation, working in partnerships. Then share out some examples.

"Partner 1, take out your writing and place it between you and Partner 2. With your partner, read through it carefully, making sure it makes sense to the reader. Think about *where* punctuation is needed and *what* punctuation to use. Go to it, detectives—work together."

I listened in, coaching partners when needed. "Look at you go, writing detectives. You are adding lots of punctuation and different *kinds* of punctuation even!

"Some of you have realized that there's not always one answer. Elizabeth and Mohammed were studying a page from Mohammed's writing. Elizabeth thought a period should go in one place, and Mohammed thought it should go in another place." I put Mohammed's piece on the overhead for everyone to notice the two options they were discussing. "Do you see how both places work? Sometimes, there is more than one place a sentence can end. The important thing is to *think* about the choices you are making. As writers, you want to make thoughtful choices."

LINK

Encourage students' partnership work before sending them off to continue editing on their own.

"Before you go off to edit your pieces on your own, look at Partner 2's writing. Partner 1, can you help Partner 2 look at just the first page? As soon as you have found three things to fix in Partner 2's writing, you can both go off to your tables and work on your own writing. After you have reread all your pages, write new ones. Just don't forget to reread *as* you are writing—to fix up your writing as you go. We won't 'save' this work till the end. Go ahead, start right now, right here!"

FIG. 6–2   Editing out *ands*

Punctuation choices are not always cut and dry. Here, I highlight the art and craft of punctuating a story—and the fact that writers will put their individual stamps on their work through their choices.

This—switching partners—is entirely optional. You will not always do this.

Building Students' Knowledge of Conventions
Punctuation and Spelling

RESEARCH IS ESSENTIAL TO UNDERSTANDING WHAT YOUR CHILDREN DO when they are asked to edit. When you look at a student's work, alone, you won't always know what to make of it. If punctuation is missing, is this because the child lacked the necessary knowledge to do better, or is this a reflection of a half-hearted effort?

I began my conference with this research move. I reflected that Isabelle was missing a lot of punctuation and asked her to address this. Right away, Isabelle identified a few missing punctuation marks. She glanced over the page and spent about 30 seconds "editing" before turning the page. When I pointed out a capital *g* in the middle of her sentence, she sighed, "Oh! I forgot."

At this point, it was clear that she hadn't carefully reread for punctuation, instead scanning casually. Realizing Isabelle was probably not alone in this, I gestured to half a dozen other writers who seemed to have a similarly cavalier approach to editing.

When the group was together, I emphasized that writers reread every bit of a text with eagle eyes, looking for ways to fix up the draft. I pointed out a few key things that writers look for, such as ending punctuation, capitalization, and the use of quotation marks. This suggestion, and directions to do this work now, in the small group, led Isabelle's work to progress (see before and after editing in Figure 6–3).

You might find that your stronger writers have mastered the second-grade standards and maybe even the third-grade ones. Gresha, another student in this small group, is a strong speller and has some good command of ending punctuation. But like all writers, she had some errors that were tough to find (Figure 6–4). Punctuating dialogue, a third-grade skill according to the CCSS, seemed a next apt step for her. You will see how she not only gained an understanding of how to identify some of her errors, but also learned some new punctuation moves, quickly.

MID-WORKSHOP TEACHING   **Using Commas in a List**

"One, two, three, all eyes on me!" I called out.

"One two, eyes on you!" the class responded.

"Writers, Tenzing found another type of punctuation that you should be thinking about as you reread your work. It isn't *ending* punctuation. She remembered the . . . comma." I put Tenzing's first page (Figure 6–5) about the carnival, on the overhead. "Will you look at Tenzing's piece of writing with me? I want to show you what she did as a writer. When she reread her sentence, it said, 'One sunny morning my sisters and my aunts my mom and my big brothers were going to a carnival.' She realized that she didn't have any commas! Commas create a list in a sentence. So, she added in commas. Look at her next sentence. Tenzing was going to write, 'There was a Ferris wheel. There was cotton candy. There was shoot the bunny.' But she didn't. She thought that would sound boring. So she made a list with commas. Listen to what she wrote, 'There was a Ferris wheel, a cotton candy store, shoot the bunny, and many other games.' Will you quickly look back at your writing and see if you have any possible lists? If so, use commas, just like Tenzing did, to separate items."

Convening a small group of kids with similar needs who are all at different levels, is one way to run a multileveled differentiated small group. This particular small group convened for less than ten minutes. It took only a few minutes for them to fix their first few pages. Slowing down and paying close attention to their writing is a great habit to begin early in children's writing development. It is also an efficient use of workshop time.

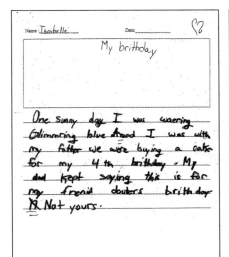

One sunny day I was wearing glimmering blue and I was with my father. We were buying a cake for my 4th birthday. My dad kept saying, "This is for my friend's daughter's birthday. Not yours."

FIG. 6–3   Isabelle's writing before the small group on editing

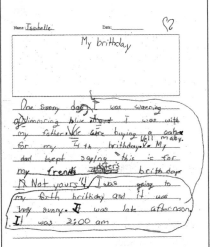

One sunny day, I was going to my fourth birthday and it was very sunny. It was late afternoon. It was 2:00 am. I was wearing glimmering blue. I was with my father. We were buying a cake for my 4th birthday. Well maybe. My dad kept saying, "This is for my friend's daughter's birthday. Not yours!"

Isabelle's writing after the small group on editing

One Sunday I was in the hospital to see my baby brother. I was so excited! "Does he have any hair?" I wondered. "I hope he is cute," I said to my dad waiting to go to the baby nursery. "I wish that too," my dad said. We had to wait long. Maybe a hundred years passed or maybe even more!

FIG. 6–4   Gresha's detailed first page of a small moment

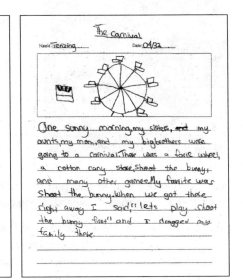

One sunny morning my sisters, my aunts, my mom, and my big brothers were going to a carnival. There was a Ferris wheel, a cotton candy store, shoot the bunny, and many other games. My favorite was shoot the bunny. When we got there right away I said, "Let's play shoot the bunny first." And I dragged my family there.

FIG. 6–5   Tenzing's detailed first page of a small moment

Any of these strategies would also work in quick and effective conferences. You might also teach your stronger conventional spellers and sentence writers how to use conventions to further their craft, for example, how the use of end punctuation impacts how a story is read, and can create excitement, slow down a small moment, or draw the reader in. Or, you might spotlight punctuation placement. Students could examine whether they are balancing longer sentence structures with shorter sentences. You might also remind students that they can use dialogue in specific points of their story to break up their descriptive sentences.

While your class is writing up a storm, familiarize yourself with your students' knowledge of spelling—the words they know how to spell with automaticity, the features of words they have under control, and what they know about problem-solving words. By administering spelling assessments such as Donald Bear's Spelling Inventory in *Words Their Way,* you can learn what things to highlight during workshop time as well as during a word study/phonics session. Analyzing the features of phonics will reveal which students require more direct support of spelling strategies.

Fixing Up Rough Drafts

Remind children that in addition to ending punctuation, they can also check their writing for spelling and comma use. Demonstrate one strategy for checking spelling in your demonstration text.

"As you reread for punctuation, you can check spelling as well. Let me give you a tip about rereading for spelling. Sometimes, there are words that you *know* or *think* are spelled incorrectly. If in doubt, circle these words as you write or reread. Before you put your writing in the 'finished for now' side of your folder, try to figure out the best spellings you can for those words. Watch as I show you how.

"Here, on my fourth page (see Figure 6–6), I have circled the word *soking* (soaking). I am going to try to spell soaking three different ways on my Post-it. Then I'll circle the best one. Later, I can look it up quickly in a book, or consult another resource. If you know how to spell this word, keep it in your head.

"I'll write *sokeing* because sometimes the *e* makes the vowel say its own name, like in *poke*. I'll also write *soaking*—like *floating*. The *a* makes the *o* say its own name, too. Or I could write *soacking*—I know words like *kick* and *lick*. The *ck* also makes the /k/ sound." I paused, surveyed the options, and said, "Show me on your finger if you think the correct spelling is number 1, 2, or 3, or my original 4. Tell your partner why.

"Many of you said #2. You said it looks right and sounds right. I agree. Now look at your own writing, circle any words you think might be misspelled, and try one of them out three different ways like I just did. Then tell your partner which looks and sounds correct and why!"

Share out a couple of ways students have learned to fix their spelling.

After a few minutes I said, "So many of you are finding *better* spellings. Mallika realized she could check the word *ocean* in the ocean and wildlife basket. She didn't even need to try out different spellings! Grace realized that one of her words was on the word wall! That is another tool to use! And Ingsel has circled words, like I did, whose spellings seem off (see Figure 6–7).

"Writers, put your Post-it notes on the back of your writing, and put your writing in your folder. Tomorrow and any day, you can add missing punctuation *and* you can also find and fix misspelled words."

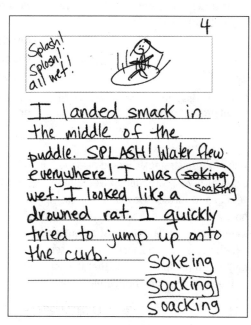

FIG. 6–6 Checking the spelling of *soaking*

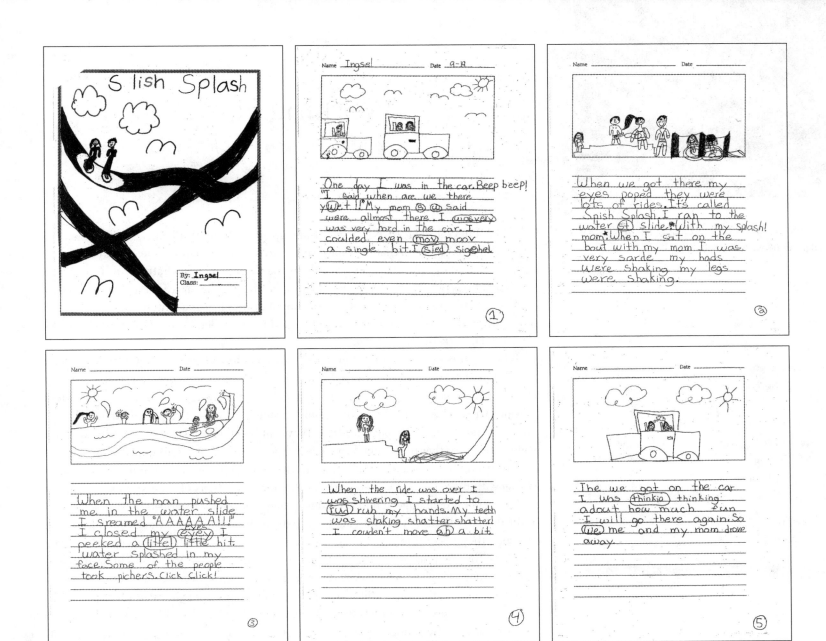

FIG. 6–7   Ingsel circles words whose spelling she will check.

Working Hard

Setting Goals and Making Plans for Writing Time

IN THIS SESSION, you'll teach students that writers get stronger by looking at their writing, making plans, and setting goals.

GETTING READY

✔ Quote from Jane Yolen (see Connection)

✔ Students' writing folders (see Connection)

✔ Enlarged copies of the Narrative Writing Checklist, Grades 2 and 3 (see Teaching)

✔ Your own writing (see Teaching)

✔ Copies of the Narrative Writing Checklist, Grades 2 and 3, one for each student (see Active Engagement)

✔ Post-it notes (see Mid-Workshop Teaching)

✔ "Things That Make Us Stronger Writers" chart (see Share)

✔ Students' writing, Post-its, and pens (see Share)

✔ "Writing Goal" chart (see Share)

THROUGHOUT BEND I, you built up your students' identities as writers. You conveyed to them that they have stories to tell, meaningful stories worth recording and reading, and then you gave them the tools and some craft moves to begin to put their stories onto the page. Again and again, throughout your teaching during this first week, you have sprinkled in bits of wisdom about how to live as a writer—how to generate and capture ideas as a writer, how to notice and magnify details as a writer, how to carry out everyday activities as a writer.

Today, in this final session of Bend I, you will teach students another important thing that writers the world over do: you'll teach them that writers set goals. Although you won't lay out specific goals for your students to tackle, you will suggest *kinds* of goals writers consider when making plans for how their writing will go. Writers decide that they will write a certain number of pages, or that they will finish one piece by a certain date and begin another, or that they will try to write in a genre that is new to them. Writers also set goals to strengthen particular skills, like crafting a more powerful beginning or ending, or writing with more detail, or stretching out the important parts of their stories.

This session challenges children to take charge of their writing—to notice what they could do even better. It also challenges them to hold themselves accountable to the decisions they make. Finally, it challenges children to take risks. Goals help us outgrow ourselves; they help us try for the selves we secretly hope to be. You want children to feel that workshop is a place where they can take risks and grow.

In this session, then, you will show children how to use the Narrative Writing Checklist to determine goals for themselves. The Narrative Writing Checklist is available in the online resources. By giving children the checklist at this stage, you convey the expectation that they work with resolve toward concrete goals to improve their work. You'll teach children a form of close reading, as you ask them to look between a description and their text, asking, "Where do I do that work? What is the evidence?"

The goal of this self-assessment is not to race down a checklist saying, "Yup, yup, yup." Instead, people use checklists when they have so many hopes that it is hard to remember them all. The checklist codifies these hopes, making it easy for a writer to remind herself of all that she aspires to do. Your expectation is that the checklist will become a source of future goals, that it will give children direction as they work to become stronger writers.

"Goals help us outgrow ourselves; they help us try for the selves we secretly hope to be. You want children to feel that workshop is a place where they can take risks and grow."

Making strategic decisions about what will make writing more powerful is the kind of analytical thinking that Norman Webb outlines in his higher-level Depth of Knowledge descriptors. The more your students assess themselves and their work, and the more opportunities they have to try out the things they decide their work needs, the more these qualities and skills of good writing will become internalized. And children, then, will indeed reach their goals.

Working Hard

Setting Goals and Making Plans for Writing Time

CONNECTION

Introduce a quote by Jane Yolen—or another quote that emphasizes the importance of setting and working toward goals.

As writers gathered, I read aloud a quotation I had written on chart paper.

> *Exercise the writing muscle every day, even if it is only a letter, notes, a title list, a character sketch, a journal entry. Writers are like dancers, like athletes. Without that exercise, the muscles seize up. (janeyolen.com)*

Quoting Jane Yolen at the start of the session does two important things. First, it gives young writers a window into their mentor author's mind—into her way of thinking about writing. Second, it gets students active right from the start of the minilesson. By inviting them to reflect on Jane's words and her process, they will reflect, too, on their own writing processes.

"Writers, over the weekend I read this quotation on Jane Yolen's website. 'Exercise the writing muscle.' Exercise?" I scrunched up my face in disbelief. "How can that be? You don't run or jump when you write."

"With your partner, quickly try to figure out what this might mean." I let kids talk for a few seconds, then gestured for Alex to tell his thoughts. "I think that it means if you write all day you will be strong," Alex said. "Will you literally have bigger muscles? What does stronger really mean? Hmm . . . " I let the question linger. "Maybe it means that your stories will be better and better. Like dancers, when they practice they dance better and can do better jumps," Grace suggested.

"Let's take both ideas," I said. "If you write everyday and exercise your 'writing muscles,' then you will become stronger writers. Maybe this means you can write longer stories! Or funnier ones! Or more beautiful ones. Maybe this means that if you work hard at writing every day, your writing will improve! Just like in sports, when you practice and exercise you get stronger, so too, you can get stronger as writers."

❧ Name the teaching point.

"Today, I want to teach you that just as dancers and athletes work hard, practice, and then get stronger, writers can do that, too. Sometimes, this work takes five minutes, sometimes a day, and sometimes even a whole month! Writers work hard to get better. Writers set goals and make plans to work toward these goals."

Today's minilesson supports a foundational skill that students will carry throughout the year and their lives—self-assessing and goal-setting. You may think that this work is too sophisticated for your second graders, but they will rise to the challenge.

TEACHING

Introduce the Narrative Writing Checklist for second and third grade, and give each child a copy.

"Let me show you what I mean. Remember last year, how you used a checklist to think about the things you were already doing as writers and the things you could work on to make your writing even stronger? Today I want to introduce you to a similar checklist, a new one with new goals on it since you are now second-grade narrative writers. These are goals you will be working toward throughout this unit and the year. I'm going to show you the second-grade goals *and* (in case some of you want to see them) the third-grade goals, too. You'll see headings. (I pointed.) The section titled 'Structure' is about how your story goes—how it is organized. The 'Language Conventions' section lists goals that will make your writing easy for your readers to read.

"There is a copy of this checklist on your rug spot so you can follow along as I read! Of course, this is just the beginning of the year, so I know you're not doing everything on this list yet. But I bet there are some things on this list you do *sometimes*. As I read the list aloud, look for things that might become a goal for you—things you think you could do more often."

Demonstrate how to compare your own writing against the checklist, setting goals for the unit.

"I finished my story about riding on the bus pretty quickly. There's one more page I haven't shared with you yet. I know there are some things I've done well, but I also suspect there are things I could improve. I'm going to look at the checklist and determine some goals that I could work toward."

I unveiled my story, written on chart paper, and said, "As I read, this group will listen to see whether I do this first item—write about one small moment, one time, and will this group of you (I gestured to a second section of the group) listen to see if I do this second item—include a lot of descriptive details about the setting? And will this group (I gestured to the kids remaining) listen to see if I did this third item—choose the action, talk, or feeling that would make a good ending. Give me a thumbs up if you hear your group's checklist item in my writing."

> Page 1: The rain had just stopped. I was sitting on the cross-town bus, staring out the window, watching the sky turn pale blue. I saw people open their jackets. I saw puddles misting in the sun. I looked up and all around me the buildings were sparkling.
>
> Page 2: Finally we came to my stop. Everyone rushed to the door. A tall man, wearing headphones, swayed his body as he barged ahead of me. Two teenage girls, arms linked, blocked my path, making a barricade. I felt crushed.
>
> Page 3: The doors opened AND I slowly walked down the stairs. Suddenly I saw a gigantic puddle. I didn't know what to do. I forgot my rain boots. I decided to jump over the puddle. I jumped.

You will probably want to read this checklist in such a way that you emphasize some things you know kids in your class are still struggling to do, things that you will want them to reach toward this month. You might also emphasize the things on the list that are similar to what they have already learned to do in first grade, and that therefore they should already be doing in their writing. The Narrative Writing Checklist, Grades 2 and 3 is available in the online resources.

Page 4: I landed smack in the middle of the puddle. SPLASH! Water flew everywhere! I was soaking wet. I looked like a drowned rat. I quickly tried to jump up onto the curb.

Page 5: Then I looked up. The sparkling buildings were hovering—high above me. Rays of sunlight danced across them. The sky was opening up with patches of blue.

I read my story aloud with emphasis. As I read, thumbs popped up across the room. Most of the third group, however, kept their thumbs down.

"Hmm . . . let's see. Based on your reaction, Group 1, I did a good job of writing about one small moment—*one time*. This is one memorable thing that happened to me, riding on the bus and getting soaked from the puddle. I saw your thumbs go up and stay up during my whole story. So I can check *that* off the list.

"Group 2, I saw your thumbs go up, too, especially when I read the part about the buildings. Yup, I definitely made sure to include a lot of descriptive details about the setting to help my readers picture what was happening. That was something I worked hard at the past few days.

"But Group 3, most of you kept your thumbs down. I know why. My story ends with a beautiful description, but the piece doesn't feel 'done' yet, does it? So that's something I could work on. It would help to include what my character is thinking, or what she says.

"Writers, see how I am going down the checklist and then looking at my writing to see if I've done these things? I could keep going—I'm sure I'll find other things I am starting to do or am already doing, as well as things I can work toward—not only in this piece, but in all the pieces I write."

Narrative Writing Checklist

	Grade 2	NOT YET	STARTING TO	YES!	Grade 3	NOT YET	STARTING TO	YES!
	Structure				**Structure**			
Overall	I wrote about *one time* when I did something.	☐	☐	☐	I told the story bit by bit.	☐	☐	☐
Lead	I thought about how to write a good beginning and chose a way to start my story. I chose the action, talk, or setting that would make a good beginning.	☐	☐	☐	I wrote a beginning in which I helped readers know who the characters were and what the setting was in my story.	☐	☐	☐
Transitions	I told the story in order by using words such as *when, then*, and *after*.	☐	☐	☐	I told my story in order by using phrases such as *a little later* and *after that*.	☐	☐	☐
Ending	I chose the action, talk, or feeling that would make a good ending.	☐	☐	☐	I chose the action, talk, or feeling that would make a good ending and worked to write it well.	☐	☐	☐
Organization	I wrote a lot of lines on a page and wrote across a lot of pages.	☐	☐	☐	I used paragraphs and skipped lines to separate what happened first from what happened later (and finally) in my story.	☐	☐	☐
	Development				**Development**			
Elaboration	I tried to bring my characters to life with details, talk, and actions.	☐	☐	☐	I worked to show what happened to (and in) my characters.	☐	☐	☐
Craft	I chose strong words that would help readers picture my story.	☐	☐	☐	I not only told my story, but also wrote it in ways that got readers to picture what was happening and that brought my story to life.	☐	☐	☐

ACTIVE ENGAGEMENT

Set students up to compare their writing against the checklist, working in partnerships to set new goals.

"Now it's your turn. Partner 1, take out a story that is on the 'finished for now' side of your folder. Look at it closely with Partner 2, and together, decide what some of your goals might be. Use the Narrative Writing Checklist to help figure out what you are already doing well. Star where you do that to show the evidence. But most of all, think about what you do sometimes, part way, that you might do every day in writing workshop to strengthen your writing." After a minute, I said, "If you are still rereading the piece, stop and talk about it now."

After a few minutes, I said, "Partner 2, it's your turn. Take out a piece from the 'finished for now' side of your folder, study it with Partner 1, and figure out your new goals."

Invite a couple of students to share their goals and reasons for choosing these.

"Writers, I'd like some of you to share the goals you are setting for yourselves. That way, you can be inspired not only by the authors on our bookshelves but by one another!"

Stephen began. "I wrote about one time. My big idea was going to Santa's Village with my mom and dad and brother, but I wrote about just when we went on the Himalaya ride and it went faster than we realized it was going to and we were all scared. But I didn't write about what anyone said. And my brother was yelling out, 'Stop the ride! Stop the ride!' and my mom was saying some stuff, too. So I should include that talk."

I gave Stephen a thumbs up and said, "Who set a different goal?"

"I did!" said Mohammed. "Mine is easy. I knew it right away. I need to work on endings. My stories always end the same way. I tell about how I was feeling. I'm gonna try ending with an action instead!"

"You're being really thoughtful about your writing goals, writers. That's how to get stronger."

LINK

Send students off to write, emphasizing their individual goal pursuits.

"Writers, you are going to be exercising your writing muscles today! Just like every day, you'll work on your stories. But today is a little different, because today, each of you will focus on a few of your very own goals. These goals can help you revise, as well as start new stories."

Providing Students with Feedback

GEOFF PETTY HAS STUDIED MILLIONS of learners in order to understand the factors that support achievement. His research suggests that students need to be engaged in challenging activities and they need clear feedback. In *Evidence-Based Teaching* (2009), Petty writes that students benefit from learning what they do well in addition to what they need to improve upon. In order to accelerate students' progress, then, we must help students work toward goals that matter, big ambitious ones, and also offer feedback—both compliments and next steps.

We've found that although it is important for us as teachers to give students compliments and teaching points, it is also important for us to teach students to self-assess so they can give this feedback to themselves. In a small group then, you may want to coach kids, saying, "Writers, look at your pieces right now. Think about what is especially strong in your writing and about what your writing needs. Do you need to slow down a small moment in your story and tell it bit-by-bit? Did you need more details? Use our Narrative Writing Checklist to help you think about your writing." Then you

---

MID-WORKSHOP TEACHING   Writers Set Short-Term Goals that Help Them Write More

"Writers, can I stop you for a moment? I want to draw your attention to something that I've noticed in our workshop today. A lot of you are thinking in your heads about what to write, but if you are to tackle your goals, you have to do what writers like Jane Yolen do—*write*! So ask yourself where you can write to in the next ten minutes. The bottom of page three? Maybe you can finish your book, reread it, and start to revise it. Then if you reach your goal, guess what you can do?"

"Set another goal?" Stephen asked.

"That's right! You can keep setting new goals for yourselves. You might set a goal of how many pages to write. Or you can set a goal for the number of books you want to write in a day or in a week.

"Right now, set a goal for yourself that will help you write long and strong! Decide how many pages—or books—you'll finish today, and write it on a Post-it note."

"I'm going to write one hundred pages!" April called out!

"I hope your hand doesn't fall off, April! Ouch! What a goal—remember you want to be ambitious and push yourselves, but you also want to set goals you can actually

reach. I see Rocio is going to write two long pages! Stephen, you made an X at the bottom of this page. Do you think you could do a little more?"

April gestured wildly for me to come over, then whispered her revised goal in my ear.

So that the class could hear, I said, "Aha, your new goal is to finish one of the books you started yesterday and then to write a couple pages of a new book? Great. That is definitely a reachable goal.

"Writers, hold up your goals so I can see them. Remember, when you accomplish your goal," I said, nodding and looking Stephen in the eye, "create a new one. I'll let you know when ten minutes are up. By that time we'll have about ten more minutes of workshop time to then reach a new goal. Are you ready?"

The kids looked at me with large grins on their faces. They held their pens close to the page as I said, "Go ahead, begin your writing. Good luck. Remember, you are aiming to write long and strong!"

After ten minutes had passed, I checked in with kids to be sure they were on target, and to help them set new goals, as needed.

might quickly move around to each student, checking in to provide bits of feedback that supports or extends their self-assessment and guides them from self-assessment to revision. In six minutes or so, you can check on each student in the small group once, then cycle through the group again to see what children have accomplished independently.

During today's small-group session, I checked in with Patrick first (Figure 7–1). "What are you thinking?" I asked, as I slid into the space next to him.

He read me his line, "When I went to Sea World I was excited."

I repeated my question to give Patrick a chance to elaborate on his thinking rather than simply reading me his writing. "So, what are you thinking? What are you going to do to revise it?"

"Stretch it?"

"Try. I will come back in a minute to see how you are doing." Moving on, I turned to Gresha (see Figure 7–2). "Let me see what revisions you've made so far," I said. Gresha's piece was a bare-bones small moment about looking for her newborn brother in the hospital. She had written one or two sentences per page. She was working on a page that earlier had read, "I looked and I couldn't find him."

"I'm trying to stretch this part out," Gresha said, pointing to the lines. "I'm trying to make the audience wonder if I am going to find him."

"Let me read what you have done." I quickly read the page she was working on.

> I looked and looked but I couldn't find him. "Look in the boy area,"
> The nurse said pointing to the boy area. I ran there. I kept looking.
> The first one wasn't him. Not even the second one.

"Gresha, I see you gave us information in the dialogue and in your actions. You slow the moment down by showing what is *not* working! I also like how you added to the picture box, 'No No No.' Did that help to remind you to stretch this page?" Gresha nodded. "You are right, this is helping to stretch out the moment. Keep going. When you finish this page, find another in your writing to stretch out the details. Use dialogue and lots of actions to do so. I'll check back with you in a bit."

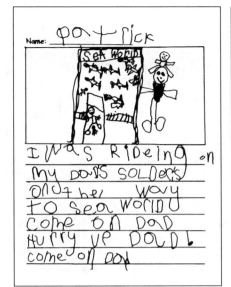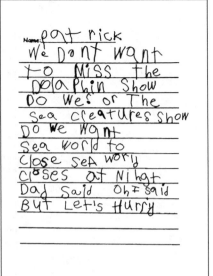

FIG. 7–1   Patrick's writing after receiving support in how to elaborate and say more about his moment.

I moved on to another child and then came back to Patrick. He had written, "I was riding on my dad's shoulders on the way to Sea World. 'Come on dad! Hurry up dad! Come on.'"

"Wow, Patrick! I love what you've done here! When we spoke earlier, you talked about wanting to revise your writing by stretching it. Using dialogue is a great way to stretch your writing, and to *show* your excitement. Keep at it. Let me hear what you will say next to show that you were excited."

"I don't want to miss the stuff."

"The stuff? Be more specific, Patrick. What do you mean by stuff?"

"Like the sea creatures! And the dolphin show!"

"Great! That is more specific. Get those details into your writing. Go!" I continued circling for another ten minutes and then sent the writers back to their tables.

One sunday I was in the hospital to see my baby brother. I was so excited." Does he have any hair? I wondered." I hope he is cute" I said to my dad waiting for to go to the baby nursery. "I wish that too" My dad said. We had to wait long. Maybe a hundred years passed (maybe even) or more!

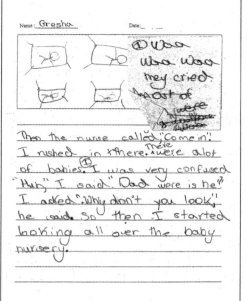

① Waa Waa Waa they cried most of were there (there)

Then the nurse called, "Come in". I rushed in there. There were alot of babies. ① I was very confused "Huh" I said. "Dad were is he" I asked. "Why don't you look" he said. So then I started looking all over the baby nursery.

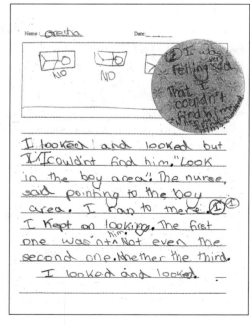

NO   NO

① I was felling very sad That I couldn't find him.

I looked and looked but I I couldn't find him. "Look in the boy area". The nurse said pointing to the boy area. I ran to there. ① ① I kept on looking. The first one was'nt. him. Not even the second one. Neither the third. I looked and looked.

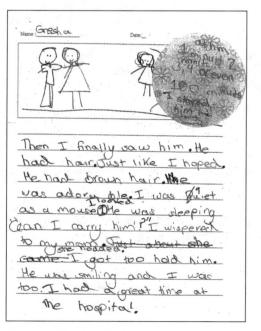

Then I finally saw him. He had hair. Just like I hoped. He had brown hair. He was adorable. I was quiet as a mouse. I looked. He was sleeping "can I carry him?" I wisperd to my mom. she nodded. Just about she came. I got too hold him. He was smiling and I was too. I had a great time at the hospital.

FIG. 7–2   Gresha's revised Small Moment story with more details added.

Learning Strategies to Become Better Writers

Introduce a chart of moves that create strong writing, and invite children to share their writing and plans with one another in pairs.

"Writers, it's time for our share session. Bring over your writing and your pen. If you just started a new piece, choose a piece you finished earlier.

"I started this 'Things that Make Us Stronger Writers' chart to help us talk and think about what you are working on as writers." I covered the bullet points on the chart, so only the title was visible. "The first three things on our chart are—read them with me." I uncovered each bullet as we read them off in unison. "'Finding inspiration from books and other authors.' We did this the first day to think of powerful story ideas in our lives. 'Writing for a long time (inside and outside of school).' Today we wrote for thirty minutes, writers! 'Writing with lots of details.' Today we can add two more: 'Setting goals using the Narrative Writing Checklist' and 'Setting goals to write more.'

"Writers have what is called a *mentor*—someone who is like their teacher! Jane Yolen once said that her husband was her greatest writing mentor. We can be each other's mentors. Mentors help you think about what you need; they also help you remember your goals. Whenever I meet with my writing mentors, they always hold me to my goals.

"Today, you and your rug spot partner will be each other's mentors. Use our chart to remind you to talk about what you did today in workshop and what you plan to work on all week in workshop. I'm going to add 'Asking for help from others' since that's exactly what you'll be doing right now."

This anchor chart can carry your students a long way, so create some excitement as you unveil it and read each bullet point. You will add on and refer to this chart throughout the unit.

Things that Make Us Stronger Writers

- Finding inspiration from books and other authors
- Writing for a long time (inside and outside of school)
- Writing with lots of details
- Setting goals using the Narrative Writing Checklist
- Setting goals to write more
- Asking for help from others

Remind students to record their goals to go on the "Writing Goal" chart.

"Before we leave the meeting area, can you write down on a Post-it a couple of BIG goals that you have as a writer? Write your name and today's date! We will hang these up on our 'Writing Goal' chart so that every now and then you can check up on your goals! By the end of the unit, you should see that you have accomplished them and gotten stronger as writers!"

① Date: ___

When I woke up my mom and dad said Were going to roller skate. I got reddy to go roller skateing.

② Name:_____ Date:_____

When we got there they gave me roller skats. I Put them on and tried with my dad.

③ Name:_____ Date:_____

I fell on my but and sied I cant do it. then I sawhim roller skating by himself.

④ Name:_____ Date:_____

And sied I can doit when he came back i told him I want to do it agien.

⑤ Name:_____ Date:_____

And I did it i told my dad I want to rollesk in the bigger area.

⑥ Name:_____ Date:_____

So he took me. Me and him rollerskatid together.

⑦ Name _____ Date _____

at first we whet slooul !!!

⑧ Name:_____ Date:_____

then we whet super!! fast we were infront everyone.

FIG. 7–3   Michael's goal is to elaborate on this piece about rollerskating with his father.

Noticing Author's Craft: Studying Imagery, Tension, and Literary Language in *Owl Moon*

BEND II

Revising with Intent

IN THIS SESSION, you'll teach students that writers revise on the go, to create a particular effect on the reader.

GETTING READY

✔ *Diary of a Wimpy Kid* by Jeff Kinney, or another book that is intended to make readers laugh (see Connection)

✔ *Alexander and the Terrible, Horrible, No Good, Very Bad Day* by Judith Viorst, or another book that is intended to make readers feel despair (see Connection)

✔ Your own writing, written in previous sessions, ready to be revised for intent (see Teaching)

✔ Post-it notes (see Teaching)

✔ Student writing folders (see Active Engagement)

✔ *Owl Moon* and *Leaving Morning* on the easel or nearby (see Link)

✔ Student writing and pen (see Share)

✔ A quote from Judy Blume—or another favorite author—who writes about revision (see Share)

T ODAY'S SESSION MARKS A TURNING POINT in the unit and an important next step for your second-graders. In Bend I you taught children how to live as writers. You suggested that, just like the masters, they could generate ideas for meaningful narratives and tell those stories in powerful ways. As children tried out some craft moves to turn their ideas into compelling stories, they also learned to reflect on their writing process, to think purposefully about their goals as writers, and to imagine ways they might outgrow themselves.

Today, you'll build on all you did in Bend I and add another layer to the work. Today, you'll teach children that writers write with particular intentions, revising on the go to be sure those intentions come through. Then you'll name out some intentions so that children have an understanding of what this means. You'll tell children that some writers aim to write stories that bring out a strong feeling or reaction in readers; they aim to make their readers laugh out loud, or feel sad. Other writers create stories that are full of beautiful images that will stop readers in their tracks—images that will make readers linger over particular lines, reading these again and again in admiration. Yet others write stories that are intended to make readers think a lot. The list goes on.

You'll discuss some stories that your children know well, imagining the intentions behind each one, and then you'll model with your own story to consider possible intentions you might bring to your story. Show children how you experiment to bring out one intention and then another, trying these on for size before settling on the one that feels right. Then ask them to think for a minute about the intentions they have for their current story. Are they hoping to create a beautiful image for their readers? To make their readers feel a particular emotion? To make them laugh? To do something else entirely?

This session, like the ones before it, reinforces the message that children are in charge of their writing. They decide what they will write about, how to tell their stories, and now, what kind of effect they hope to have on their readers. This kind of purposeful, thoughtful decision making not only supports higher-level thinking skills, it also conveys to children that they are no longer the little kid writers they once were. They have grown and so, too, can their writing. Of course it also conveys to them that they aren't alone as they make these decisions. They can learn from other authors, noticing how they bring out their intentions.

"This kind of purposeful, thoughtful decision making not only supports higher-level thinking skills, it also conveys to children that they are no longer the little kid writers they once were."

This session also continues to build up children's talking and listening skills. Rather than thinking about their intentions in isolation, children will talk through their ideas with a partner. Not only does this offer students a support system, it also encourages them to engage in thoughtful discussion. When children must explain their thinking and hopes to each other, they end up reflecting on their writing in meaningful ways. Then, too, this kind of dialogue relays to students that they are accountable not just to their own writing projects and goals, but also to their partners and to the community of writers to which they belong. Giving children a sense of responsibility in the workshop is as essential to building their identities as writers as is giving them rein over their writing projects.

Revising with Intent

CONNECTION

Show students examples of various published books that are written with different intentions, some meant to be funny, some meant to be sad, and so on.

"Writers, do you remember on our first day of writing workshop when we imagined how authors like Jane Yolen and Angela Johnson come up with their story ideas? Remember how we guessed that they probably recorded moments that mattered to them—ones that stood out from everyday happenings—and then turned those into stories?" The kids nodded and I continued. "All of you have been doing the same thing. You've been generating small moment ideas about meaningful moments in your *own* lives, jotting those in your Tiny Topics notepads and then weaving them into stories. I've been poring over these every day, marveling at how you describe moments like dancing at your first recital, learning to tie your sneakers, welcoming a new pet, saying good-bye to a grandparent. It's incredible how you've found such personal moments to write about. As I was reading your work, I looked up at my bookshelf at home and do you know what two books popped out at me? I saw this one," I held up *Diary of a Wimpy Kid*.

"Oh, I know that one! I saw the movie!" Tajwar shouted out.

"My brother is reading that book at home," Lindsay chimed in.

"It's a popular book," I said. "It is the kind of book that was written to make us laugh! It's what I would call, 'a funny book.' Right?"

"LOL!" Gabriela called out.

"I like that, 'a laugh out loud story.' Thanks for that suggestion, Gabriela."

"Right next to *Diary of a Wimpy Kid*, I spotted *Alexander and the Terrible, Horrible, No Good, Very Bad Day*." I held this book up for the class to see. "This is a more serious book. Reading it, I worried for the main character. What could we call this kind of story?"

I was quiet for a moment, ready to jump in with my own idea, if needed. But then Eric said, "An 'oh, no! story'!"

◆ COACHING

Many fiction books begin in a familiar setting. Where the Wild Things Are starts with Max getting into trouble of one kind and another, and being sent to his room without any supper. A familiar story: Readers can nod, and think, "I've been there." Only after this beginning does the story take off on a wild and magical ride. In minilessons, too, it's often the case that the story starts on familiar ground. Yes, indeed, students have learned how authors have come up with story ideas. Home territory. But in a pinch, this minilesson takes kids to terrain they have not yet traveled. It's a wild and magical journey.

"Yeah!" the kids called out. They suggested other stories that fit into these categories. Before we got too far off track, I said, "These two books made me think of my own book that I was writing and of all your books, too! It made me think, 'What kind of book am I trying to write?'

"This is a question that writers around the world consider. *Most* writers at some point in their writing process ask themselves this.

Share with students what you were trying to do as a writer in your demonstration piece.

"When I wrote my story about riding the bus and getting drenched in the puddle, I knew that it was a good story to tell and I cared about that moment—it stood out to me. But if you were to ask me, 'What are you trying to do as a writer?,' I am not quite sure what I would have said. I'm not sure if I was trying to write a 'laugh out loud story,' a 'feel sorry for me' story, or even just a 'look how beautiful' story. The truth is, I'm not sure *what* I intended or tried to do as a writer. I just wanted to tell a good story. And that's okay—for a *first* go."

❖ **Name the teaching point.**

"Today I want to teach you that writers revise—on the go—not just to add in details, but to bring out a certain meaning, or a feeling in their reader. They think, 'What am I trying to do as a writer?' They consider how authors they admire have done the same thing. Then they revise their *own* writing, trying out a few different ways to see which one feels right and matches what they want their readers to take away."

TEACHING

Reread your own writing aloud, voicing various intentions you have for its effect on readers.

"Let me show you what I mean. I'm going to revisit my piece about riding the bus and ask myself, 'What am I trying to do as a writer?' Hmm, . . . So what *am* I trying to do? What do I hope my reader gets out of this piece? Do I hope my reader feels like she's in a beautiful place, like the one Jane describes in her story? Do I want my reader to feel a particular emotion? Or what?"

Demonstrate how you decide on an intention—making the story funny—and revise accordingly.

I unveiled my story on the easel, and ran my eyes over it, thinking out loud. "You know, I think one thing I could try is to make this a story that is really funny! I mean, falling into a puddle is hilarious! I could rewrite parts—especially on this page," I pointed to page 4, "to make my reader laugh more." I could write:

> I stumbled and fell off the first step like a boulder in a rockslide. I saw myself getting closer to the huge puddle. "Uh oh!" I said to myself. And then I crashed. There was water in my ears, my eyes, even in my boots.

Of course, most writers start by writing for themselves. First, writers must care enormously about a topic so that they will want to spend time writing about it. But always, writers know (or hope, anyway) that eventually there will be a reader at the other end picking up their stories. And so writers also write for readers.

Revising writing takes energy and thought. Oftentimes it takes writing yet more to really see an idea through. When writers get tired, their words sometimes feel lazy and they lose the meaning they are trying to capture. In this lesson, your goal is to reenergize your writers. You convey that revision isn't something one waits for at the end of the process; rather it is something that writers do constantly, throughout their work on a piece. By demonstrating on a "perfectly fine" piece of writing how one can revise an entire part in a few different ways to bring out various emotions or ideas, you not only show your students how to lift their level of writing, you also raise their concept of what revision is and how it works.

Notice that I don't actually write these versions. If I did, this minilesson would be much too long.

The kids laughed.

"That's kind of funny, huh?" I said.

"Yeah, you wrote an 'LOL story'!" some kids called out. "It got funnier and funnier."

Demonstrate how you generate an alternate intention and again revise accordingly.

"Yes, I exaggerated the situation to make it funny. But I'm not sure that's my intent. Hmm. . . ." I opened my book to the beginning and then flipped quickly to the end. "You know, when I saw those buildings sparkling all around me, I felt really happy. Maybe I want my reader to pay attention to how lovely the place was. If I want to do that, I could write what I saw with lots of details. I could say:

> Then I looked up. The sparkling buildings were still there, high above me. Rays of sunlight
> danced across them. The sky had patches of blue.

"Let me try one more thing. What else could I try? I could show how I was feeling sorry for myself—the crowded bus, the big puddle, getting wet. This would make the reader feel that this was a terrible, horrible, no good, very bad day. I could add to my second page:

> Everyone was on top of me. I was afraid I wouldn't make it off the bus! An elbow jabbed me.
> Then the doors started to close and a man pushed in front of me. I wanted to scream, 'OPEN
> THE DOORS!'

"Does that sound like I am having an awful day?"

Everyone nodded vigorously.

Model considering the possible intentions, and then choosing one for your revision.

"Phew," I said, wiping my brow. "Those are a lot of choices to consider. Do you see how weighing those options helps me think about how to revise with more purpose? How I considered what I want my reader to get out of my story? I didn't try just one thing, did I?"

"No!"

"I tried *three* things! I imagined three things I might be trying to do, and revised to bring those three out. You know what? I think what I *really* want my reader to know is that I started off grumpy but then felt so happy when I saw those sparkly buildings."

This is more demonstration than is needed. I kept it in here just because I liked it, but the point is conveyed without this final example.

By considering several intentions behind your own story, you convey the expectation that students will explore several possibilities themselves. This experimentation challenges students to consider the effect their writing will have on readers and to then make thoughtful, deliberate revisions.

Debrief, restating the teaching point.

"Writers, now that I've thought about three possible purposes, I can revise my story so that it does what I want it to do. Remember, first writers write, thinking about a story that matters to them. And then they think, 'What am I trying to do as a writer? What do I want my reader to take away?' and they revise, to bring out that intention."

ACTIVE ENGAGEMENT

Set students up to consider their own intentions for previously written pieces.

"So writers, are you up for the challenge? Let's try it, right here, right now. Ask yourself, 'What am *I* trying to do as a writer in *my* piece?' You will want to consider a few possibilities, not just one! Open up your writing folders and take out one piece of writing to look at right now." As kids reread their pieces I called out some voiceovers to guide their thinking.

> "Are you trying to tell a sad story? A funny one? An exciting one? Think, 'What kind of story am I trying to tell?'"
>
> "Think about what you want your readers to feel."
>
> "If you have thought of one way your story might make your reader feel, think of another possible one. Say, 'Or maybe . . . ' When you have two or three ideas, put your thumb on your knee so that I know you are ready."

I gave kids who hadn't yet put up their thumbs a little advice and then said to the whole class, "Remember, it doesn't have to be the *perfect* idea, just try and imagine your writing going a few different ways. It's the imagining that matters! Be flexible—explore different options! Now share what you tried with your partner. Partner 2, you are going to go first. Partner 1, encourage Partner 2 to say more than one way the story could go."

Share examples of different intentions that students have for their writing.

"Justin told Isabelle that he could try to give his magic show story a *surprise* ending story! What an interesting idea. He also thought he could try to make it funny. Isabelle and I both agreed—those are two ideas that would work well in his story! Right now, Justin is going to revise his piece to make it a 'surprise' ending story. Makes me so curious as a reader!

"Tenzing told Gabriela that she could try to make her story about playing with her dog a sad story because the dog died just a little while ago. Gabriela thought she might do what I did in my sparkly building story. The story could start one way, and end another. She might begin by showing how beautiful her dog was and then end showing how sad she is that he died."

If the work of this session seems a bit above your kids' heads, don't be surprised. They'll make something out of it, and the concept will be one they revisit often.

LINK

Remind students how powerful it is to consider what they want their readers to think and feel as they read their writing.

"As you get started on your work today, remember that you will capture moments and stories to tell that matter. Sometimes it helps to write the story first and then reread it thinking, 'What am I trying to do as a writer?' Be the kind of writers who write with purpose so that your readers come away with certain feelings, images, or reactions to your stories—just like Angela, Jane, and all of our favorite writers do." I gestured to the other books that were up on the easel.

"They don't just tell a story; they tell it in ways that get readers to see and feel specific things. That's the power of strong writing. I can't wait to see what you all try today! Today, when I ask you the question, 'What are you working on as a writer?,' it will mean something different, because now you know so much more."

CONFERRING AND SMALL-GROUP WORK

Coaching Writers to Walk the Walk and Not Just Talk the Talk

EXPERIENCED WRITING TEACHERS know that opening a conference by asking, "What are you working on as a writer?" is one way to encourage writers to fill you in on what they have been trying to do. When you ask this question, however, some children will not know how to answer and will simply tell you about the *content* of their writing: "I'm working on my story about the time I went to the farm." It is essential, then, that you teach your children what you mean by the question, "What are you doing as a writer?" Tell them, "I didn't mean what you are writing about; I meant, what are you working on as a writer. Are you revising? Are you working on spelling a hard word, are you rereading your writing to make sure it makes sense and sounds right?"

If children have a hard time telling you what they are working on, reference some of the charts in the classroom. "Are you trying to write with details?" you can ask. "Or are you working on an ending that brings the story to a close?"

As I was observing one of the writing tables, my eyes strayed to Alex who was revising a story from the red-dot side of his folder. The story told about an experience he had had at the Halloween parade. Before I began the conference, I'd noticed that Alex had already made a few revisions to this text. Now he was rereading his entire draft. "Alex, how is your revision work going today?" I began.

"Oh good, I'm trying to slow down the important part of my story," Alex said, assuming his role as a writer and adopting the language that accompanies that role.

"What a grown-up answer! That is so much more specific than saying, 'I am writing about when someone took my picture at the Halloween parade!' What you said helps me understand what it is that you are working on as a writer. Now, when you say you are trying to 'slow down the important part,' what do you mean?" I asked, even though, of course, *I* knew what the expression meant.

"I mean that I am going to add more words so it takes longer to read it—like the reader has to slow down and read it because there's so many important details."

MID-WORKSHOP TEACHING
Conferring with a Partner in a Meeting Spot

I briefly interrupted the students, who were working diligently at their writing spots. "Writers, I know that some of you are eager to talk to your partner about what you are trying to do as a writer; you want advice. But some of your table-mates are finding it hard to concentrate! Over here"—I walked over to the meeting area, where there was a round table set up—"near the meeting area, are a table and two chairs. I also have a timer you can set. If you need a writing conference with your neighbor, the two of you can come over to this table, set the timer for three minutes, and talk to each other. This way you can continue to think with a neighbor about what you are trying to do as a writer. If you see other kids at the table, wait till they are finished with their conversation. Then you can take your turn."

"Can you show me in your writing where you are doing that?"

Alex read his story out loud to me, then pointed to the end of the text and said, "Here I want to say more stuff about the person who was taking my picture, because that was the part where I said, '*No!!!!!*' really loud."

"What will you say to slow that part down?"

"I don't know. I'm stuck. I want to add on here, but I don't know what to add."

"Well, let's think. Why is this part important?"

(continues)

"Because . . ." Alex paused. I gave him time to think. "Well, because I was dressed up like a vampire, right? And vampires are not supposed to get their picture taken ever—something bad happens, but I forget what, so I didn't want the guy to take my picture."

Before I taught Alex a new strategy, I complimented the work he had already done. I also wanted to be sure to name for him what I was going to teach him, and why. By naming my teaching point and giving him a process, my expectation is that he would be able to replicate these steps again and again in future writing. "Alex, I love how you reread your writing, and found a specific place where you wanted to do your revision work. You have a plan, and that is so smart. Now that you know where you want to make your revision, where you want to slow down your writing, you can reread that bit of the story and try to get a clear picture of what was happening in your mind. This way, you can remember all of the important details. You can slow the story down in *your* mind first, before you slow it down on your paper." I demonstrated this for Alex, using his own piece to do so. Then it was his turn. "This is your story—keep thinking out loud about what you see when you slow that important part down. What happened next? Keep going with the story."

Alex tilted his face and told the story as if in a trance. "I saw a person put his hand up. There was a camera in his hand. I put my hand up. I said, 'Noooo!'"

"You did it! You got a clear picture of what was happening. Do it again, and this time, think about yourself as a vampire. How do vampires act?" I said, raising my arms up slowly. "Say it like you are writing the story, Alex."

Alex continued. He began to envision bit by bit just what was happening and even used a scary, vampire voice. "Oh, Alex, this is so much more exciting and clear. Now I understand what was going on when you shouted 'No!' at the guy. This is so funny. Let's get it down on paper. Go back to where you first started. 'I saw a person put his hand up. There was a camera . . .' Keep going."

I moved on to my next conference with Gabriela. After a few minutes I looked up and watched as Alex finished rewriting his first page. Before he started the third page, I reminded him of what he had just done, so that he could replicate it again. Then I turned back to Gabriela to begin the next part of my conference with her.

Name: Eric

This is me win
I Lost A towt
At The prk on
A niys day

it WAS A Hit
samr DAY I WAS
iN The PArk
PrAtsrn My Biek
win I Git
tiyd I WAGld
my towt it
DADN+ CAM out
I PLD my towt
it CAM out sieisy

FIG. 8–1   Eric works on adding details to the beginning of his writing.

Using a Storytelling Voice

Have students read their writing in small groups, using their voices to show their intentions.

"Writers, I want to give you a chance to share before we wrap up your writing for today. Bring your pen and a piece of writing in which you either *tried* a couple of things *or* you *thought* about trying a few things."

"Rows one, three, and five, will you and your partner turn to the writing partnership directly behind you? The four of you will make a mini writing circle. Each of you will share one place in your writing where you either tried to bring out a few different intentions, or thought about ones you could try. As you share, learn from each other."

After the kids had talked for a few minutes, I voiced over, "Pause!" and pretended I was pressing a DVD player.

It is extremely important to provide time for students to share their work and get feedback from their peers throughout the writing process. It is more likely that students will listen to their peers and make changes to improve their writing if they participate in this process more than once.

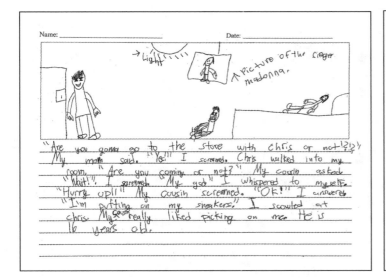
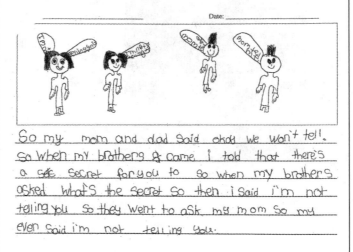

FIG. 8–2   These two writers practiced storytelling and using dialogue. Here are two excerpts from their writing.

Share out a couple of children's intentions.

"Writers, Stephen did something bold. He took a risk! He tried something he had never done before. He tried out Justin's move—a *surprise* ending! Justin was his mentor. If you were a risk taker today, too, or if you learned from someone in your group, congratulations. Keep sharing! Read the parts out loud!"

After a few more minutes, I called "Pause!" again. This time, kids mimicked my action with their fingers. "Elizabeth said that she was trying to make her story super scary! And then she read it in a 'scary voice.' As you read your next story, if your intention is to make the reader *feel* something, use your voice. Group members, afterwards, talk about whether the words the writer used help you feel that way! Play!" I used my "press" signal on my hand to indicate the next partner should go.

Share a quote from Judy Blume—or another favorite author who inspires the idea of revision.

"Judy Blume, one of my favorite writers, once said, 'The first draft is a skeleton—just bare bones. The rest of the story comes later with revising.' Over the next few days, you are going to be breathing more 'life' into your skeleton stories. We are going to study how writers make places, and people, and surprises come to life, and how they make us feel powerful emotions!"

Close Reading

Learning Writing Moves from a Text

IN THE FIRST BEND, you taught students ways to get ideas for stories from the world around them. Then, you taught them to think about their intentions for their stories, to guide their revision. Today, you offer up the entire Library of Congress collection to them as a writing resource. Of course, you don't want to overwhelm children with too many steps, too many choices, and too much new material all at once—you don't want them trying to sip from a fire hose! So, you'll start by using just one book as a writing resource, one book they already know well: *Owl Moon*.

By studying *Owl Moon*, using an inquiry approach that will allow your students to take the lead, you and your class will name the effect certain lines of text have on readers. You will then scaffold students' work in naming, as best they can, how the writer achieved that effect. As you do this, you and your children will create a chart of craft moves Jane Yolen uses that they, too, can try in their own writing. (This chart is an adaptation of Katie Ray's in her book *Wondrous Words* (1999).) Though you are starting a chart with lines from *Owl Moon*, in future sessions you'll undertake the same work with other texts by other authors. In Bend III of this unit, you will have given children enough scaffolding in using books as writing resources that they will be able to find their own mentor text, find some powerful parts, name the effect these have, and figure out what they, too, can try to create that same effect.

You will notice that the format of this minilesson does not follow the typical structure of teacher demonstration followed by student active engagement; rather, you and your students will be working together during the teaching to investigate the question, "How does the writer makes this part of her text so powerful?" If students experienced writing workshop last year or the year before, they will be primed for this inquiry-based minilesson.

You may question an inquiry approach here. Indeed, it is a lot to expect second-graders to notice what makes a section of text powerful and to describe how that effect is achieved, and even more still to expect them to take that abstracted knowledge and apply it to their own burgeoning work. And yet, we have found that when you raise the bar for what you expect children can do, they are more than happy to surprise you with their efforts. Along

IN THIS SESSION, you'll teach students that writers use books as writing resources. They study different parts of books and think, "Could I write like this?"

GETTING READY

✔ *Owl Moon* by Jane Yolen, or another mentor text. Powerful parts of the text should be marked with Post-it notes

✔ "Learning Writing Moves from Our Favorite Authors" chart, started with headings, to be filled in during the minilesson (see Teaching)

✔ Writing folders, pens, a few Post-it notes (see Share)

the road to learning to do this work, children will stumble. Some will copy parts of the mentor text word for word. Some will emulate exactly the parts of the mentor text that do *not* create the effect they are going for! Some children will write words that seem to be completely unaffected by the mentor text. Without fail, this will happen, and it does not mean that this session is too hard for your writers.

"What a gift you give your youngsters by teaching them how to use every text in the world as a resource to help them communicate their ideas with more strength or more beauty or more power!"

What it does mean is that the learning of this session does not happen instantaneously for most learners. You will need to coach and offer scaffolding, and as we've seen again and again with children from every walk of life, they will learn to use the texts around them as teachers.

For today, then, you and your students will make a chart to anchor children's close study of this text, you'll discover some craft moves, and describe how to re-create these. You will also name and identify for students a process that writers go through as they study texts. In naming this process, you will position your students to continue this work as independent writers and readers. In the next few sessions following this one, we focus more on helping children learn ways to apply the craft moves they've discovered to their own writing.

Close Reading
Learning Writing Moves from a Text

CONNECTION

Ask children to recall the intentions they came up with yesterday for their stories.

"Writers, yesterday you tried out a few different ways your story might go—you decided your story might be sad or funny or make the reader feel sorry for you—or something else. Close your eyes for a moment and remind yourself of one of the intentions you have, one of the ways you are trying to affect your reader. What do you want your reader to take away? Thumbs up when you remember."

Instead of asking children to remember your teaching, you are asking them to remember the work they did. This conveys the important message that they are in charge of their writing decisions.

Tell children that to create an intended effect on readers, they can study books to learn how.

"Making your story have a particular effect on readers—making them feel a certain way—is really, really hard work. Adult writers spend their whole lives doing that work. Because this is such a tough job, writers definitely need all the help they can get.

"When you need help as a writer, you can always study other books and use them to teach you how to do special things with your writing. You can learn how to affect your readers. You can learn how to bring out a feeling, or how to make your reader laugh out loud or have a particular thought like, 'Wow!' or 'I didn't expect that.'"

TEACHING AND ACTIVE ENGAGEMENT

❀ **Name a question that will guide the inquiry.**

"Today, writers, we are going to do an inquiry. Together, we are going to look at powerful parts of our mentor text and investigate, 'How did the author write like this?' so that we can try this out in our own writing."

World-class standards place a great priority on children growing up aware of the choices that writers make and able to talk about how those choices support the central idea of a text.

GUIDED INQUIRY

Set children up to study a powerful part of the mentor text and to name the effect it has. Remind them of the questions they will ask.

"Let's try this work together as a class, right now, with *Owl Moon*. We are going to look at some powerful parts and ask the question, 'How did the author write this part?' We are going to notice *what* is powerful, name *why* it is powerful, and then figure out *how* to do it! We will ask what, why, and how!

"Let's take a look at *Owl Moon* now, at the parts we marked the other day as being really powerful. And, remember, let's ask the questions, '*What* is powerful?' and '*Why* is this part powerful?' And then, of course, we need to think about *how* the author does this.

"So, *what* powerful part should we study first? A part where there is a strong feeling? One that makes the reader think something interesting? A part with a beautiful image . . . ?" My voice trailed off, leaving open other possibilities.

Isabelle's hand shot up. "At the beginning, on the first page I think that it is very beautiful. It is very quiet and I like the words 'a sad, sad song.'" I put that part up on the overhead. When all eyes were on me and the room was silent, I read aloud the first page of *Owl Moon* slowly.

> It was late one winter night
> long past my bedtime,
> when Pa and I went owling.
> There was no wind.
> The trees stood still as giant statues.
> And the moon was so bright
> the sky seemed to shine.
> Somewhere behind us a train whistle blew,
> long and low, like a sad, sad song.

Scaffold students' work in naming and discussing *how* the author makes this part of the text so powerful.

I paused to let the words sink in. "Isabelle, I'm thinking about *why* this part is beautiful. It makes me feel the place all around me, almost like I'm there! Does it have the same effect on you all?" There were nods. "So that is one reason *why* it is powerful."

"Now, let's see *how* Jane does it! Let's all read it one more time, to ourselves, in our minds. This time, ask yourself, 'How did she make this so powerful—in this case, how did she make it so beautiful? What did she do that I could I try in my own writing?'"

Opening up your teaching like this, posing an inquiry question, presents some potential challenges. You may be thinking, "What if my kids don't say anything?" or, "What if they only read the part aloud and don't actually name what makes this part powerful or interesting?" The truth is, anything could happen. Your students may surprise you by naming something that didn't even occur to you. Try to think of this inquiry as just that—an inquiry. There is no one right answer. Meanwhile, you, of course, are students' greatest scaffold. Be ready to give suggestions and a demonstration about how you think about the text—and have some ideas of your own about the craft moves Jane uses and to what effect. The idea is to teach kids to be inquisitive, to be researchers. You'll be surprised how quickly kids catch on and follow your lead.

It helps to cite a substantial portion of the text when considering the craft moves a writer makes to evoke a particular feeling, or to paint a picture that lures the reader in. This way there is more to see and notice and discuss. Here—already on the first page—Jane does so much to create a setting that pulls her readers in. Always, we want our children to draw from a repertoire as they write—whether this is a repertoire of strategies for generating ideas or a repertoire of techniques to create a particular effect. Being able to see how a professional writer does more than one thing, in more than one place, will solidify this concept for your young students, making it more likely that they see more as readers, and do more as writers.

The children read silently. Then I said to the class, "Turn and discuss what you noticed Jane Yolen doing here. Try to use lots of words! Name *how* she makes this part powerful. What is her technique? What has she done that you could try?" As children began talking as a whole class, I revealed the following chart, and filled in what we'd come up with so far:

Learning Writing Moves from Our Favorite Authors

WHAT is powerful ?   WHY is it ?   HOW is it done ?

page 1 of <u>Owl Moon</u>   feels like you are there

I reread the lines again, and again raised the inquiry question, "*How* did Jane make this part powerful?" I waited patiently for responses, scanning the group for willing volunteers.

Finally, Tenzing broke the silence. "She writes about the sky shining and the moon being bright and I think that is what makes it beautiful."

"Ooo!" Grace blurted out, raising her hand up high. I pointed to her to share. "Yeah, it's like she tells us the setting and what it looked like!"

Challenge children to see and name more on the page. Share out some examples.

"I'm going to write on our chart what you two have said." I did and then asked, "Is that the *only* thing she did here to give us this clear, beautiful image? What else do you see? Turn and talk, quickly!"

"She tells you about the train whistle," Leslie said.

"Yeah, and that it sounds like a sad, sad song," Mohammed added on.

Channel children to name what the author has done that they, too, can do.

I asked, "If *you* wanted to try this in your own story, what would *you* do? What if your story doesn't have a train? Hmm, . . . Could you do this anyway?"

"Yeah, because it's just like writing what you hear!" Alex said. I added that to our chart.

You are inviting children to develop a never-ending resource—books—that can enrich their own writing for years to come. For some, it will be new to think not only about what a text says, but also about how the text is written. Welcome children's rough approximations, knowing the lessons you teach in the next few days will continue to challenge them for years. Giving students multiple tries reinforces their learning. Maybe the first time, they weren't able to notice or name anything. Now, with the support of hearing each other, they might take on some of the language of their peers.

> ## Learning Writing Moves from Our Favorite Authors
>
> **WHAT is powerful?**
> page 1 of
> <u>Owl Moon</u>
>
> **WHY is it?**
> feels like you
> are there
>
> **HOW is it done?**
> names exactly what
> the character:
>
> - sees
> - hears
> - feels

"She calls the trees giants!" Gabriela called out.

"They are like statues!" Chloe said, gleefully.

Name what the students have done and link this work to their writing. Remind them how studying a text in this way is like having another teacher.

"Giant statues. The trees are like giant statues? I think you are right that these techniques make this part powerful. And you could use these too! Notice that Jane also makes a comparison. Comparing the trees to giant statues helps us get a picture of just how big and still those trees were.

"Writers, there is so much more we could say about this part! Studying a book this closely, really paying attention to not only *what* an author does but *how* she does it, is a great way to learn craft moves that you can use in your own writing. If you want to make readers feel almost like they are there, in your story, tell people what a character sees, hears, feels, you have a teacher. If you want to use a comparison, you have a teacher.

Set children up to learn another craft move from a mentor text, using the same steps. Scaffold the process as needed.

"Let's read another powerful part—who has a suggestion?" Hands shot up.

"I know!" Patrick said, crawling onto his knees. "Let's talk about the part before the owl shows up, when the dad calls out whoo-whoo-whoo!"

"Okay, and what makes that part powerful, Patrick?" Patrick froze and gave me a shrug. I wondered if he'd just wanted to make the owl call. But other kids looked eager, so I said, "Who can help Patrick? Lots of you seemed excited when he named this part. So what makes it powerful?" I turned to that page and held it up.

"It's exciting, because you wonder if the owl will actually show up! But you don't know yet!" Fabiha said.

"I think it's because it makes us hope, hope, hope to see the owl," Gresha said.

"Yes, I see this. We do wonder if the owl will appear, so it keeps us wanting to read, *and* we hope right along with Jane's characters that it will," I said. "I'm going to add that to our chart."

Learning Writing Moves from Our Favorite Authors

WHAT is powerful?	WHY is it powerful?	HOW is it done?
page 1 of <u>Owl Moon</u>	feels like you are there	names what character exactly: • sees • hears • feels makes a comparison
Right before owl arrives in <u>Owl Moon</u>, when the father calls out to it	you wonder what will happen next, and hope things turn out a certain way	• uses actions and images that show a character hopes for something

"Now, as I read it aloud, follow along with me, and then you and your partner will think about it together. After I read, I will be quiet as you and your partner answer the questions, 'What did the author do to make us feel, *whoa, what next* and *I hope, I hope, I hope?*' 'What is her technique?' She doesn't say, 'Reader, wonder about this. Hope for that.' Since she doesn't do that, how does she do it?" I read the part out loud, slowly.

> I sighed and Pa held up his hand at the sound. I put my mittens over the scarf over my mouth and listened hard: "Whoo-whoo-who-who-who-whooooooo. Whooo-whoo-who-who-who-whoooooooo." I listened and looked so hard my ears hurt and my eyes got cloudy with the cold. Pa raised his face to call out again, but before he could open his mouth an echo came threading its way through the trees. "Whoo-whoo-who-who-whoooooooo."

As children talked, I listened in, coaching here and there. After a couple minutes, I signaled for their attention. "What did you figure out? Thumbs up if you want to share."

"We could tell that she wanted to see the owl because she listens so hard." Elizabeth said.

"Yeah, she listens and looks so hard her ears hurt and her eyes get cloudy!" Tenzing added.

"Imagine listening and looking so hard your eyes and ears hurt! Those actions—and images—definitely show us she is hoping to see an owl!"

I looked around the class, signaling for someone to add on or to offer another idea. "Also, she gets you to wonder because the owl doesn't show up right away," Gresha said. "Like there's an echo but you don't see anything. It's like a clue."

"Oh! And a little bit past this part, you see the shadow before you see the owl," Grace added.

"Hmm, . . . so Jane gives us signs of the owl before it actually arrives—could we use Gresha's word, 'clues'?" The kids nodded.

"Oh!" Stephen called out. "I see another Jane Yolen!"

"A Jane Yolen? You mean a move that Jane Yolen makes in her writing? Professional writers call these 'craft moves' but I like what you call it—a Jane Yolen! Okay, tell us!"

"Well, it's not just this part, but the whole book," Stephen said. "I think Jane stretches out the story. She could have made the owl come sooner, but she made us wait."

"Wow. You are so right. Jane stretches out her story over all these pages (and I flipped through the book's pages). And we don't see the owl until almost the end. She saves the big thing for later."

"Let's add these craft moves to our chart quickly, before we forget them. You just did some sophisticated thinking work. Bravo!"

This is, indeed, sophisticated thinking. Your students may notice different things, and that's just fine. You can always steer them to see and name particular moves, if you're so inclined.

Learning Writing Moves from Our Favorite Authors

WHAT is powerful?	WHY is it powerful?	HOW is it done?
page 1 of <u>Owl Moon</u>	feels like you are there	names what character exactly: • sees • hears • feels makes a comparison
Right before owl arrives in <u>Owl Moon</u>, when the father calls out to it	you wonder what will happen next, and hope things turn out a certain way	• uses actions and images that show a character hopes for something • gives clues that something might happen • stretches out the story. The big thing doesn't happen right away.

LINK

Recap the craft moves that children have figured out from today's work. Suggest they try these in their own work, if their writing calls for it.

"Writers, now that we've figured out several of Jane Yolen's writing moves, ask yourself, 'Does one of these moves match what I am trying to do in my own writing—my intentions?' See if there is a spot in your writing where . . .

◆ You want readers to feel like they are almost there—right with the character

◆ You want readers to wonder what will happen next, and to hope things turn out a certain way

"If you do a 'Jane Yolen' in your writing today, be ready to share how you did it at the end of our workshop."

"On the other hand, if your writing doesn't need any of the things we've found in Jane's work, you might want to study another part of *Owl Moon*, and find something else she has done as a writer. Then you can pocket that lesson, just like we can pocket these lessons, forever and ever—to use when you need them.

"Or, you can do other things that your writing needs. There are lots of options. Quickly tell your partner what you will work on today in the workshop."

I called on a few kids to share their "mini-plans" with the class before sending students off to write.

Addressing Common Challenges Students Face When Transferring New Strategies to Their Writing

IN YOUR ROOM TODAY, YOU MAY DISCOVER some students have begun to write their own owling books, while others have "borrowed" Jane Yolen's words. That is, their attempts to mimic her craft moves may end up more as imitations of her content—and a trifle closer to the original than is helpful to them as writers. Any author study runs this risk, and especially one done with young children. Your challenge, then, is to help students who fall into this category find inspiration in the beauty and power and craft of the mentor author's writing while holding fast to their individual story intentions and ideas.

In the following conference, you'll see how I work with Grace, one writer whose story is patterned a little too closely after *Owl Moon*, to help her think through how to make her story (see Figure 9–1) more her own, so that she transfers Jane Yolen's *craft moves*, not plot and structure, to her writing.

"Grace," I began, "I see that you have made a story that is *very* similar to *Owl Moon*. Can you walk me through your thinking? Which of Jane's craft moves did you use in your own story?"

"Sure. One thing I did was use details to make it feel like you're in the story," Grace said.

"Can you show me where, exactly, you did that?" Grace pointed to sentences she'd written describing the setting.

"Indeed, those details do put you right into the moment," I said. "Keep walking me through what you did. Are there other craft moves of Jane's that you used in this piece?"

Grace named a few, and was especially excited to share this one: "I wrote, 'When you go hiking, you have to be quiet.' And then here, 'When you go hiking, you have to be brave.' That's like how Jane says, 'When you go owling, you have to be quiet.'"

(continues)

MID-WORKSHOP TEACHING
Using Repetition to Show Your Big Idea

"Writers, can I press *pause* for a moment? Chloe and I were just discussing her story, and trying to figure out what her big idea was. She thought she wanted to show just how exciting her first day of swim class was. Then she thought about what the *big* idea was in *Owl Moon*, what Jane was trying to tell us by writing this story. Do you know what she said? 'How to go owling.' She thought that Jane wanted us to know what it feels like to go out in the night and try and look for an owl! I asked Chloe which parts especially get you to feel that. Listen to the parts she chose and think about what Jane Yolen is doing as a writer. What craft move is she using—that is, what is this 'Jane Yolen'?"

I began to read aloud three short excerpts from *Owl Moon*.

> But I never said a word.
> If you go owling
> you have to be quiet
> and make your own heat. (page 11)

> When you go owling
> you have to be brave. (page 13)

> When you go owling
> you don't need words
> or warm,
> or anything but hope. (page 29)

"Do you hear or see something interesting that Jane is doing in these parts?"

"It's like it is the same!" shouted Mohammed.

(continues)

"Yeah," Elizabeth chimed in. "She keeps saying 'owling, owling, owling.' Like a refrain in a song."

"Think about what Mohammed and Elizabeth are saying—she keeps saying the same thing again and again, like a refrain. Listen." I reread the three parts. "What is she doing with these parts?"

"It's like she repeats it again and again but a little differently," Chloe said. "Like each part tells you something else you have to do when you go owling."

"Isn't that interesting? These three parts are all about what to do when you go owling. By repeating 'When you go owling . . .' and then giving us another tip, it's almost like Jane is saying, 'Hey, Reader, listen up. This is important.' It's like she's highlighting her big idea."

I wonder if I could try out something similar in my story about falling into the puddle to show what I want my readers to know! Hmmm . . . oh, I know. I want people to know that they should move more slowly—especially on crowded buses. I bet I could come up with something to repeat a few times to let people know that! Chloe is also thinking about how she can use repetition to share her excitement over her first swimming class.

"Right now, will each of you turn and talk to your neighbor about what you want your reader to know in the story you're working on now? What is your *big* idea? If you don't know, see if your neighbor can help. Some of you might want to try what Jane did as a writer and use repetition to show this idea. Or you can go to a different part in *Owl Moon* and ask what, why, and how. Take a couple minutes to talk and I'll meanwhile add repetition to our chart."

Taking advantage of the teaching opportunity, I said, "Wow, Grace, you really got the sound of Jane into your writing. In fact, that sentence is exactly the same as the one Jane repeats in *Owl Moon* except that you swapped the word *hiking* for *owling* and a deer for Jane's owl. Do you see that?"

Grace nodded.

I moved on to my teaching point. "Grace, when you try out a mentor author's craft moves, you have to be careful to write *your* story and *your* words."

I paused to let this sink in, then said, "Let me ask you something. Why did you put Jane's line into your story?"

Grace looked stumped at first. Then she said, "I just liked how it repeated. It kind of stayed in my head. Like a song."

"I agree with you, Grace. It's a catchy line and it works to bring out something important about Jane's story. Repetition does that. So here's another tip: If you want to borrow this craft move, ask yourself, 'What line—or refrain—could I write that will show why my story matters so much to me?' Do you want to do that now, with your story about the deer?"

"Um . . . I don't know," Grace said.

Her hesitation confirmed my thinking that Grace's story about hiking had been more an experiment in emulation than anything else. I added, "You know what, Grace? You don't have to write about an experience in the woods in order to use Jane's craft moves. That's the beauty of craft; it works in all different kinds of stories. You could use repetition, like Jane does, *and* include details that put the reader right into the story in one that's all your own!"

Grace looked relieved. I wondered if maybe she hadn't even gone hiking with her family, but didn't ask.

"Any idea what your next story will be about?" I asked. Grace told me that she wanted to write about going skating with her mom.

"Great! Think about the skating rink and the time you spent there with your mom. Ask yourself, 'What do I want to show about that day?'"

After discussing the feeling she hoped to convey in her piece, Grace and I imagined a couple of different ways the beginning might go, replicating some of Jane Yolen's craft moves, but aiming to spotlight new ideas and different feelings—ones that were unique to Grace's experience.

In Grace's second piece, notice how she attempts to use a few of the craft moves she admires in Jane Yolen's writing. They don't all work perfectly, but Grace now has a better sense of how to transfer what she is learning to another topic, one that is true of her experience (see Figure 9–2). Notice, too, how much more personal this piece feels; it's evident that Grace is writing about something that matters to her.

One sunny day, the sun was shining bright. Me and my uncle went hiking. We walked up the mountains. It was morning and we were hot. The cars honked like talking over the dogs. The trees were melting like snow, from the beaming sun. When you go hiking, you have to be quiet or else animals will run away and make you roll down the hill. My uncle had a kind of camera that has no sound for animals. The rabbits whistled through the wind. It seemed peaceful when you heard the silence. When you go hiking, you have to be brave or else, maybe an animal can attack your mom or dad. Then you will be alone. Hiking is about all of nature around you. When I took a step forward, a cute deer jumped in front of me. The deer wouldn't even let go of her eyes at me and my uncle. I finally saw an animal that was so beautiful. My uncle took a picture of the deer. Click! Click! Click! quietly it said. My uncle and I turned around to go home without saying a word.

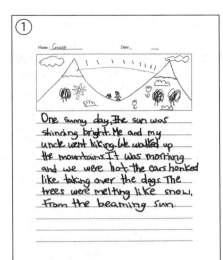

FIG. 9–1 Grace's first version of a small moment story that minics Jane Yolen's *Owl Moon* text very closely.

You may also find that you have students who copy the examples straight out of *Owl Moon*. You will want to give them opportunities to see how other students make it their own. You may even decide to show them how a second writer, like Angela Johnson, does this same work, but in a different way. Then you will want to coach students to try the same thing in their own writing.

On page 4 of her story (Figure 9–3) Leslie had written, "The water felt crisp and cold and moved like waves pushing to me like a sad, sad song." As I approached Leslie in the conference I asked her what she meant. She said, "Well it was really quiet." I probed further to sort out my confusion, "The pool area was quiet?"

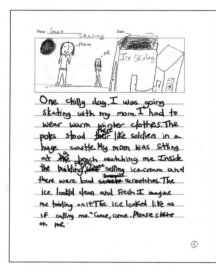

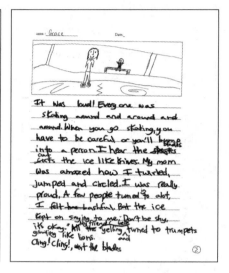

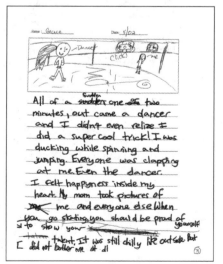

FIG. 9–2   In Grace's second version of this small moment story, she attempts to use craft moves from *Owl Moon*, yet writes a personal, true story from her own life.

One chilly day, I was going skating with my mom. I had to wear warm winter clothes. The poles stood there like soldiers in a huge castle. My mom was sitting at a bench watching me. Inside the building people were selling ice cream and there were loud screetches. The ice looked clean and fresh. I imagine me twirling on it. The ice looked like as if calling me. "Come, come. Please skate on me." It was loud! Everyone was skating around and around and around. When you go skating, you have to be careful or you'll bump into a person. I hear the blades cut the ice like knives. My mom was amazed how I twirled, jumped, and circled. I was really proud. A few people turned in to a lot. I felt bashful. But the ice kept on saying to me, "Don't be shy, it's okay." My friends were yelling and turned to trumpets growling like lions. Cling! Cling!, went the blades. All of a sudden, one or two minutes, out came a dancer and I didn't even realize I did a super cool trick! I was ducking while spinning and jumping. Everyone was clapping at me. Even the dancer. I felt happiness inside my heart. My mom took pictures of me and everyone else. When you go skating, you should be proud of yourself to show your talent. It was still chilly like outside. But it did not bother me at all.

"Yes," she replied.

"How does that fit with a sad, sad song? Why did you choose those words?" Instead of telling Leslie that she couldn't just take words from another book and put them in hers, I wanted to learn from her about her writing process.

"I don't know. I wanted to compare it. Like how Jane Yolen did."

"Well, that is an idea for this part. I am sure you can do what Jane Yolen did, just in your own way. You don't need to compare it to a song. You can compare it to something that reminds you of the pool area and how it was quiet. The waves were gentle?"

"Kind of."

"Well, let's both think about possible comparisons and find which one will match the best! You could say, 'The waves were pushing me like . . .'" I waited to see if she was ready to jump in. A few seconds ticked by and I filled in the silence, "a snowplow pushing me over." Leslie got ready to write. "Oh, no! That's just one try. We have to find a few to find one that matches. A snowplow? Is that gentle?"

"No! But the wind is."

"How would that go?" I waited again. From the table next to ours, Chloe piped up, "Like the wind blowing the leaf."

"Oh, thanks, Chloe, that is gentle. Leslie, let's keep thinking . . . "

"Like the swing?"

"Say what you mean," I waved her in like she was stealing home.

"The waves were pushing me like my mom pushes me on the swing? Or on the merry-go-round?"

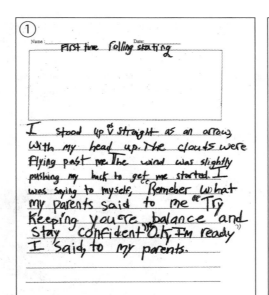

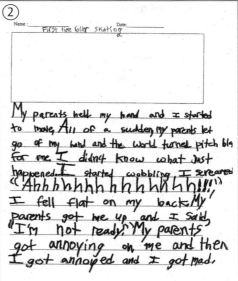

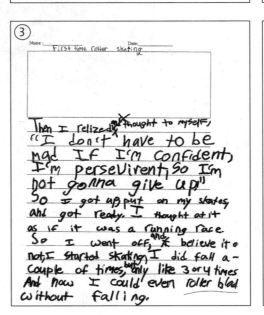

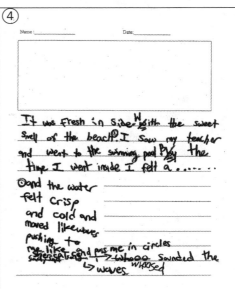

FIG. 9–3   Leslie's attempt to revise her writing to match her moment and experience better, rather than lift specific words or text from *Owl Moon*.

"Wow. Those are comparisons of your very own. Which one matches the best? You decide."

Leslie chose the merry-go-round because its motion reminded her of the waves pulling her around. As she wrote down her words, I said, "Maybe there are other places where you wrote the same words as Jane Yolen, where you can now write your own description." I waited as Leslie reread her piece. Soon she found another part where she had written, "Whooo." I looked at her and said, "Mmmmm?" She quickly crossed it out and wrote, 'Whoosed.' Then she looked back up at me. I pointed to the page. Leslie read on, making decisions about what to cut and what to keep.

Trying Out Craft Moves

Acknowledge the difficulty in separating the mentor author's topic from her craft moves.

"Bring your writing folders, a pen, and three Post-it notes to the meeting area. Before our share, show your partner any 'Jane Yolens' you tried today!

"Writers, today you have reached what I call a 'tipping point'—you are changing as writers! You are noticing everything—everywhere! That is what writers do!"

"I also see that many of you are now rethinking your stories. Some of you have even said to me, 'Do I need to write a story about seeing an owl?' And that is a good question. How do you do some of the same things that Jane does, without writing her story?! How many of you felt after reading Jane's story, *Owl Moon*, like you wanted to write a story about winter?" Some thumbs popped up.

"That's okay, writers, it happens. I used to write all these stories about my dog. Like when I would give my dog a bath. Then all of a sudden my best friend started writing stories about her dog—but she didn't even have a dog! She always had the hardest time coming up with a story, so she just copied me. She wrote about giving her dog a bath, taking him for walks—her *pretend* dog, Herman!

Ask students to Post-it the most important parts of their stories, in partnerships, in preparation for trying out more craft moves in tomorrow's workshop.

"Over the next few days, you are going to learn how you don't have to *copy* writers in order to try their same craft moves in your *own* pieces. The first step you took at studying craft was reading *Owl Moon*, remember? Now you'll do the same thing in your writing—with your partner. Reread your writing—like a reader. Use Post-it notes to mark up some of the most important parts of your story. This way you'll be ready tomorrow to learn how to use what Jane does in *Owl Moon*. Partner 1, be the first reader. Partner 2, help Partner 1 find the most important parts in his or her writing. Then, swap turns."

After children had a chance to do this, I shared out a couple of examples.

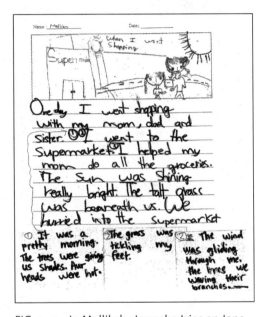

FIG. 9–4   In Mallika's story, she tries on Jane Yolen's craft move of describing what she sees and feels. She describes more of the setting on this first page.

Learning to Write in Powerful Ways

Trying Out Craft Moves Learned from Mentor Authors

IN THIS SESSION, you'll teach students that writers make their writing more powerful by trying out craft moves learned from mentor authors.

GETTING READY

✔ Student writing from the prior session's Share (see Connection)

✔ Your own writing, about a shared class experience, marked with Post-Its in places where you could try out craft moves (see Teaching and Active Engagement)

✔ "Learning Writing Moves from Our Favorite Authors" chart (see Teaching)

✔ Student writing folders (see Link)

✔ A piece of writing from a student who would like feedback (see Share)

I N TODAY'S SESSION, you set children up to try one of the craft moves that they noticed in the class mentor text the day before. Although your students will have experimented doing this work in the previous session, and will be eager to do it today, it will be challenging for some to go from noticing a craft move to applying it to their own writing. We suggest, therefore, that you take time during your demonstration to carefully model the steps involved in this work. Notice that the story we use is one that describes a shared class experience. This is intentional. Children will have an easier time following what you do (during the teaching) and then trying it themselves (during the active engagement) when they themselves have experienced the story you tell.

The real challenge will be showing children how to mimic a craft move (in this case one move involves naming what a character sees, hears, and feels, and the other, making a comparison that helps the reader feel like he or she is there). You don't want children to simply lift lines from the mentor text into their own pieces, or to write stories that are thinly veiled versions of the mentor.

On the other hand, don't fret if children do, at first, copy the mentor text in these ways. All of us who strive to write like an author we admire have at times found that person's style or voice or even story lines creep into our writing.

Do help children ask the sorts of questions of themselves and their partners that will guide them to use the mentor author's craft moves in powerful ways. You'll see, for example, that in this session's active engagement, I ask children to put themselves back into the moment when they discovered the class fish had died, to think about exactly what they saw and heard, how the room felt, and how they said good-bye to the fish. I ask them to think about what intentions we all might have for writing a story like this one—and to think about how they could use Jane's craft moves to realize this.

Welcome your children's approximations in this session, knowing they won't all produce masterpieces. Meanwhile, also push them to think, feel, recall, and record like master writers.

Learning to Write in Powerful Ways
Trying Out Craft Moves Learned from Mentor Authors

CONNECTION

◆ COACHING

Begin by asking children to mimic your actions exactly. Then ask them to come up with their own actions, modeled after the ones you show them.

Before gathering the children in the meeting area, I said to all of them, "Writers, follow me." I lifted my arms above my head. Children's arms shot up in the air. I slowly moved my arms down in front of me, palms facing up. Students looked at each other in bewilderment and followed. Next, I pretended to make a snowball and toss it up in the air, making a dramatic catch. The kids mimicked my movements. "Wow, you all are such skilled mimics. You are really studying each move I make.

"Now, I want you to try something a little different. Watch me as I do something else, and then take what I do and give it your own 'spin'—that is, do it in your own way."

I made a series of hand motions that were too complicated to exactly mimic and then said to the class, "Your turn!" Arms moved, hands twisted every which way, and then laughter broke out.

"Nice interpretations, writers!

"Table monitors, get the writing caddies and set up for workshop. Everyone, bring the piece you Post-ited yesterday and take your rug seat now."

Remind students of the work they did in the previous session, looking carefully at the crafting techniques used in *Owl Moon*, and then marking places in their writing where they could give these a go.

"Yesterday we looked *really really closely* at *Owl Moon* to think about what parts of Jane's story were especially powerful and to think *how*, exactly, she wrote those parts in her story. We noticed *what* she did, talked about *why* she did it, and some of you even tried out some of her 'moves.' We noticed that Jane made us feel like we were right there with her, pulled us right into her story, and that she got our hearts beating quickly just before the owl showed up—she made us wonder what was going to happen next and hope for something, right? And then you marked places in your own writing where you might try out some craft moves to make your writing more powerful, like Jane's.

Here, I begin by warming up children's mimicking skills. It is essential that they be able to spot a "move" and to try it out as best they can. They'll be approximating Jane Yolen's moves in a similar fashion.

Here, I am not looking for children to copy my move, but instead to try it out, making it their own. Children will, of course, have fun doing this, but it meanwhile also conveys an important message. As young writers, we do mentor ourselves to more seasoned writers, trying to learn from them, to do as they do. But we also find our own *voice, our* own *moves. You'll want your children to feel as much like apprentices as they feel like creators.*

"Today in our writing workshop you are going to use what we studied in *Owl Moon*, in your own writing, in your own ways! You're gonna try out some of her 'moves.' You're gonna do a 'Jane Yolen,' as Stephen calls it.

"Earlier, I told you to bring the piece of writing you Post-ited yesterday with you to the rug. Will you hold it up for everyone to see?" I waited until all the kids had their pieces up in the air. "Mentoring yourself to Jane Yolen doesn't mean that you each write your own version of *Owl Moon*. And it also doesn't mean that you'll use Jane's exact details, or her exact words, or her voice. You aren't going to *copy* Jane Yolen. But you *do* want your writing to be powerful like hers. You can learn how to do the same things she does, and create your own spin!"

❖ **Name the teaching point.**

"Today I want to teach you that one way to make your writing more powerful is to try out craft moves that a mentor author uses. You can find a spot where you are trying to make your writing powerful in the same way that your mentor author has made her writing powerful, and then you can try the same moves in your own piece, in your own way."

TEACHING

Model using the "Learning Writing Moves from Our Favorite Authors" chart as a resource for making your own writing more powerful.

"Let me show you how I take what we learned from Jane and apply it to my own writing. Let's look back at our 'Learning Writing Moves from Our Favorite Authors' chart and also at this piece I wrote about our goldfish dying.

"Remember how Tenzing was about to feed Goldie when she noticed she wasn't moving? I'll start us off. I have the first draft of the story here," I held up a booklet with just a few lines of print started with rough sketches and a couple of words to hold the meaning of each part. "When all of you put Post-it notes on parts of your writing where you might try out a craft move, I did the same thing. I marked up some of the parts of our class story as well."

I put the story up on the overhead. "Listen to how it goes so far." I read aloud:

"Tenzing, time to feed the fish!" Elizabeth said.

We heard Tenzing crying. We all went to the fish tank. We saw our Goldie, floating on top of the water.

"What should we do?" Mallika said. We looked at each other and waited and waited. Then we all said goodbye to Goldie and went back to work.

Lots of people grow up believing that they don't have what it takes to be a writer. "Writers," they think, "have very special talents." In a writing workshop, we try to help children realize that in fact, the skills and talents writers draw upon can be learned. This is a powerful, lifelong lesson. In this way, we try to lure all children into believing that becoming a great writer is possible for them.

You will, of course, want to pick a story from your classroom, an event of some kind that was slightly dramatic. Maybe it was a passing of a class pet, a fire drill, being late to lunchtime, or being caught in the rain. One class in San Diego wrote a class story about a hummingbird that flew into their room, and another teacher in Seattle wrote a story about being caught in the rain on the playground. Each of you will find the class story to bring to life in your classroom.

"This is tough. I don't think there's enough of a picture to help readers imagine themselves there. I used a Post-it to mark this part where we were all standing near the fish bowl. That's an important part because we were very upset, but that doesn't come through. I think I might add in a bit about what I saw or heard"—I pointed to that part of our chart under How—"so that readers will feel like they are there with us, around the fish bowl, feeling what we feel. Just like Jane did at the very beginning of *Owl Moon*! Do you think that would help?" The kids bobbed their heads yes.

"Hmm, . . . Let's take a look at our chart." I thought out loud. "At the beginning of *Owl Moon* Jane names what the character sees, hears, and feels, to help readers feel like they are right there with her. That's what I want to do with our class story, make readers feel like they are right there. So I'm going to do the same thing that Jane did at the beginning of *Owl Moon*."

Learning Writing Moves from Our Favorite Authors

WHAT is powerful?	WHY is it powerful?	HOW is it done?
Page 1 of <u>Owl Moon</u>	feels like you are there	names what character exactly: • sees • hears • feels makes a comparison
Right before owl arrives in <u>Owl Moon</u>, when the father calls out to it	you wonder what will happen next, and hope things turn out a certain way	• uses actions and images that show a character hopes for something • gives clues that something might happen • stretches out the story. The big thing doesn't happen right away.

"I could say something about what the room *sounded* like to show how worried we were. It was completely silent, remember? We were really worried. What else do I know that has that same kind of sound—silence? Silence, like just before a storm, or silent like a mouse, or silence like snow falling onto a tree? Hmm, . . . Which one might be best to use? How about this?

> The room was filled with silence, like just before a storm. No one spoke.

"I made a comparison, like Jane's trees that she compared to giant statues. See if you can imagine yourself there," and I read the revised draft.

> "Tenzing, time to feed the fish!" Elizabeth said.
>
> We heard Tenzing crying. We all went to the fish tank. The room was filled with silence, just like before a storm. No one spoke.
>
> We saw our Goldie, floating on top of the water.
>
> "What should we do?" Mallika said.
>
> We looked at each other and waited and waited. Then we all said goodbye to Goldie and went back to work.

"Writers, thumbs up if that second version pulls you in to the story more—if you feel like you are there, at the back of the classroom." The kids gave me an enthusiastic thumbs up.

"Did you see how I matched our class story with a part in Jane's story where I wanted to do something *similar* to what she did? Then I tried it out!

"Those additions make a big difference. I didn't talk about pointy trees—there weren't any of those in the classroom! But I *did* borrow Jane's craft move to make us feel like we were there—I made a comparison to help readers imagine how the room sounded."

ACTIVE ENGAGEMENT

Recruit children to help you try out craft moves in another part of your writing.

"Now let's try this together. Let's work on the part when we saw Goldie floating. Listen:

> We saw our Goldie, floating on top of the water.
>
> "What should we do?" Mallika said.

"Okay, now let's think, 'What do we want our reader to feel? Happy?'" The kids emphatically shook their heads no. "Excited?" I pressed.

Tenzing was up on her knees. "No no, we were really sad," she said, and the rest of the class nodded their heads in agreement.

"Aha, sad. So let's hold that in our heads as we write. Again, let's try to make sure we write in a way that makes our readers feel as if they are right there. What should we say then? Should we say what the fish food looks like? Thumbs up if you think that's important for our reader to know." The kids giggled. "No? Okay, how many of you think it's important to say more about what Goldie looked like when we found her?" Thumbs flew up in the air.

"I agree. It feels important to show that she didn't look quite right. Because that's when we knew something was wrong. Okay, turn and talk to your partner about what you could add. Let's try and use the same craft moves. Let's say what we saw that could also show what we were feeling. Try to say more than one thing. Hold up a finger each time the two of you come up with a new idea so that I know how many ideas you have. Think, 'What would Jane do here to help make the reader feel like he or she were right there in the classroom with us?'"

You'll notice that we provide steps in today's active engagement to help scaffold students' writing during this part. You can decide whether this type of scaffolding—trying each step first together—is necessary for your particular class. You may instead opt to have kids just add into this part, orchestrating the steps together.

Revise your shared writing, based on students' suggestions.

After a few minutes I said, "One two three, eyes on me. Writers, I heard some really clever suggestions just now. Ramon and Mallika said that Goldie's belly was *up*, not down. What a strong, sad image. I can see her now, belly up. And Stephen and April said that Goldie's eyes were kind of blank—as if they were staring at nothing. Let's see if we can get those two things in."

> We saw our Goldie, floating on top of the water. She wasn't swimming. She was belly up in the tank. Her eyes were blank. They stared at nothing.

"I think we're getting there, writers. Readers would definitely feel like they were right there, seeing poor Goldie belly up, with blank eyes. But— our ending isn't as clear, is it? Did we really go right back to work? Or did we do anything else?"

"We said goodbye to Goldie," Kenzy suggested.

"Yes. And did we shout, 'Goodbye, Goldie!'?"

"No, we whispered it," Mohammed said.

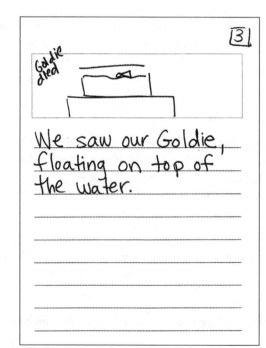

FIG. 10–1 Goldie Died story, before revisions

"We whispered goodbye . . . ," I repeated, letting my voice trail off. "Channel Jane and talk to your partner about how to add on to the ending. Ask yourselves, 'Is there anything else we might add to get the reader right there with us?'"

I left a space of silence as children worked, then I reconvened the group and shared out some of what I'd heard. We added on and soon our class story went like this:

> "Tenzing, time to feed the fish!" Elizabeth said.
>
> We heard Tenzing crying. We all went to the fish tank. The room was filled with silence, just like before a storm. No one spoke. All of the children were huddled around the bowl, shoulder to shoulder. We could barely hear each other breathe.
>
> We saw our Goldie, floating on top of the water. She wasn't swimming. She was belly up in the tank. Her eyes were blank. They stared at nothing.
>
> "What should we do?" Mallika said.
>
> We looked at each other and waited and waited.
>
> We whispered goodbye to Goldie. She didn't move. We were quiet like the night.

I read the revised class story out loud. "You are getting the hang of it. You're thinking about what you want your reader to notice and feel. You're using craft moves you learned from *Owl Moon*. Your words help the reader feel like he or she is there, with you, seeing and hearing what you see and hear. This is a sad story, isn't it? Some stories are like that."

This shared text is another exemplar for the classroom, and will be useful both for you, as you teach, and for students, as they write. You can use this shared class writing during conferences, small groups, mid-workshops, or even share sessions. Students, meanwhile, can compare their writing to this text, looking between the two to determine if they are using craft moves to similar effects, and as a reminder of ways to add to and revise their own work. It helps to give students a vision of the amount and variety of revision you expect them to try out.

LINK

Ask children to look through the writing in their folders and make a plan for the day's work.

"Quickly, look through your writing. Do you have any places in your story that you marked yesterday where you might add more words to help your reader feel like he or she is there in the story with you? Think about what kind of story you are writing—is your story sad? Funny? Exciting? Happy?—and then see if you can bring that out—probably in a way we learned from Jane. You can use the chart to remind you—Jane did it by telling about the things her character saw and heard. You might even come up with an interesting comparison like she did! Start here in the meeting area. As soon as you have tried it once, take your writing back to your writing spot and keep going!

"If you don't think you have a part where you are trying to do this in your writing, that is okay. Find another kind of part. Maybe you have a part that you are trying to make suspenseful, just like Jane did! You could try out other craft moves in your own writing, too.

Remind students that they can look at books for ideas to make their writing more powerful.

"Remember, whenever you are trying to make your writing more powerful, mentor authors can help! You can turn to a book, like *Owl Moon*, and find a part that matches and try to use similar craft moves to help you do whatever you want to say in your story."

Notice that I refer to authors in general, rather than just to this author. For example, I say, "We were trying to be like our mentor author," or "We can learn many things from Angela Johnson, or from any author." I am trying, in subtle ways, to be sure that students learn that they can study and emulate any author.

Supporting Writers of All Abilities to Use Mentor Texts

YOU WILL MOST LIKELY NOTICE SEVERAL things in your students' writing after this session. First, in some students' pieces, there will suddenly be an overuse of the particular craft move you have taught. In some cases, this won't help improve the work at all. In fact, sometimes it will cloud the piece. Don't panic. Remember, in order to learn anything, it is necessary that your students first approximate. This allows you to then give them feedback on their attempts. Remind your students that writers are selective about when, where, and how they use craft moves. They think, "What am I trying to show my reader?" and then they decide whether a particular craft move will do the trick.

Other students won't use the craft move you have taught. They'll continue writing with no evidence that they have learned something new. It could be that these students get so wrapped up in their writing that they forget to try out the new move. Or it could be that they don't understand how to use the craft move in their writing. Treat each student case by case, investigating the reason and then either providing another demonstration, as a reminder, or pulling kids in this category into a small group in which they practice the craft move on a shared-class piece of writing and then have a go at it in their own work. Another option is to give these students a second opportunity to do a close read of the mentor text. Pull a small group together and ask kids to look for other places in the text where the mentor author's writing invites readers into the world of her story, making them feel like they are there. The group might even name new ways they notice she has done this.

In addition to these two scenarios, your advanced group of writer, who have had some success using the craft moves you have taught so far, may be ready to think about your teaching in a more sophisticated way. Up until now you've taught children how to add details that show what they see and hear around them—to paint a picture with their words. Your more advanced writers may be able to create setting in their writing with the added component of mood.

(continues)

MID-WORKSHOP TEACHING   Unearthing a Craft Move to Support a Strong Bond between Characters

"Writers, I need to stop you! This small group and I"—I gestured to the kids sitting at the kidney-bean-shaped table—"just found a new 'Jane Yolen.' We found something else Jane does as a writer! Books really do give you so many ideas for how to make your writing more powerful! We noticed that the story creates the feeling that there is a strong bond between the father and the child that night. The story is powerful in part because we feel that bond; we feel the child noticing her father and her father's ways. So we looked to try to see *how* Jane created that feeling.

"We realized that Jane doesn't just tell us what the daughter sees and hears all around her in the woods. She also tells what the daughter *and* the dad were doing in this story. It's almost like a seesaw in some of the parts of the story! First the dad does something, then the daughter does something. Sometimes it is even the *same* thing that they do. If you look at the beginning of page 7, you'll see how Jane writes about *both* characters! I'm not going to reread aloud right now, or even add it to our chart, since you could do either of those things on your own. This is something you can come talk to anyone in this group about, if you want to create that feeling of a strong bond between characters in your own story.

"You can study *other* parts of *Owl Moon* as well, to find more ways to make your own writing go how you'd like it to go. Remember, books can give you many different ideas for your writing. Then you can think together about how it could go in your piece!"

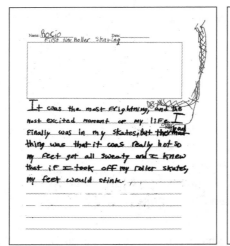

It was most frightening and the most excited moment of my life. I finally was in my skates. But the bad thing was that it was really hot so my feet got sweaty and I knew that if I took off my roller skates my feet would stink.

FIG. 10–2 Rocio's first draft of her first page (before small group) in which the details show little concern about what she is trying to show.

It was most frightening and the most excited moment of my life. I finally was in my skates. The sidewalks were cracked. The sidewalk was bumpy. Roots were sticking out the trees and on the walk. The cars were swooshing by me and the honks made me get distracted, so I lost my balance. But the bad thing was that it was really hot so my feet got sweaty and I knew that if I took off my roller skates my feet would stink. My parents said, "Just keep you're balance and you just have to stay confident."

FIG. 10–2 Rocio's revised first page (after small group) in which she tries to stretch out the setting to show her feelings.

Rocio and Isabelle were two writers I pegged as ready to do more. They were both starting new pieces during the time of this session. In a group conference, I reminded them of what they had learned about painting a picture with words and asked them how they planned to do that in their new writing. Rocio, ever confident, said, "I think I did it already!" I read her first page (see Figure 10–2), and quickly realized that she'd been a little bit hasty in her claim—but because she'd been successful up until now, I decided to push for more nonetheless. I said, "Isabelle and Rocio, here is the challenge.

First, let's look back at Jane Yolen's opening and think about what she did to make us feel like we are in her story. Then, let's look at Rocio's opening and decide if she has done the same thing."

Together, we read aloud Jane's opening to *Owl Moon*. The girls reiterated what the class had noticed—that Jane tells her reader what the woods look and sound like. They agreed that it was easy to imagine themselves in this scene because there were really clear images, like the "trees as still as giant statues."

"Okay, now let's look at Rocio's opening," I said. "What do you notice that's like what Jane did, and what's different?"

"She tells us that she's scared and excited, but I can't really picture where she is," Isabelle said. "I can imagine her feet all sweaty, though," she said, giggling, "but I'm not sure what's all around her."

"Hmmm . . . interesting. So Rocio included a detail about her feet. We could even say that the sweating is because she's scared and excited! But you can't yet imagine where Rocio is, right?"

Isabelle nodded.

"Rocio, what do you think?" I asked.

Rocio admitted that she hadn't done quite as much as Jane in her story beginning to paint a picture.

"Jane stretches out the setting," she said, wisely. "It's like she doesn't just tell you one thing about what she sees and hears. She keeps adding to it. And there's even a feeling in the train whistle. It sounds like a sad song."

"That's a really good description of how Jane opens her piece," I said. "Yes, she stretches out the setting, and she does it in a way that readers not only feel like they're in the story, they also feel an emotion. Writers call that mood."

"Both of you, take a look at your writing. Ask yourself, 'What mood—or feeling—do I want the reader to feel?' Then see if you can find a way to give your reader that feeling through the words you use to paint a picture."

Then I added, "Try to really stretch out your setting, like Jane does."

As the girls worked, I noticed that Isabelle had used Jane's exact metaphor. I pointed to it and whispered, "Remember to borrow Jane's craft, not her words."

"Oops," Isabelle said. Then she said, "Oh, I know!" and crossed out the words *stood still as statues.* After thinking for a while, she changed the line so that it read: "Zombies, witches, and monsters were everywhere and creaking houses were completely dark."

"Terrific revision," I said. "You've definitely created a scary mood!"

Then I looked at Rocio's and said, "The details you've added about the honking cars and the cracked, bumpy sidewalks work so well to put us into your sweaty skates!" The girls giggled, but it was clear that they'd gotten the point.

Both of these students tried to create tense, frightening moods in their pieces—though one is the kind of fright that comes from all things spooky, while the other is the kind of fright that comes from trying to perform—and facing challenges. If these students were older, I might talk to them about the differences between these two "scary" moods, but for students of their age, this lesson is enough.

Obviously, your children will write entirely different pieces, but the teaching of this conference will still apply to your more sophisticated students who are ready to think about setting in a deeper way.

One dark empty night of Halloween me and my dad went trick or treating. I was dressed as lady gaga with a bow tie on my head and a black suit. The moon was dark it was very scary. Zombies, witches, and monsters were everywhere and creaking houses were completely dark. Nothing but decorations. I holded on my dad's hand very tightly so I don't be sc sc sc scared. I kept saying I'm not scared. I'm not scared. Until I heard voices near my head. That time I was scared.

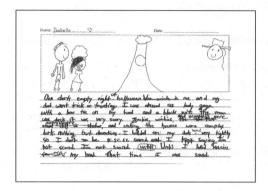

FIG. 10–3   Isabelle's revised first page (after small group) in which she has added details about the setting to show her feelings.

Providing Feedback to Peers

Have students provide feedback to writers who feel like they need advice from readers.

"Writers, take a second to reread what you wrote. If you forgot a punctuation mark, or a word, fix it up right now. When you have read up to where you are now—put a Post-it there and come over to the meeting area.

"Writers, Chloe said that she would love some feedback from the class. She is trying to help her readers imagine themselves in her story. I have Chloe's story. We are going to study it together and think about what she might add to help her readers imagine that they are there! She has marked a part in her writing which she thinks would be a good place to paint a picture for the reader. Tell us your thoughts, Chloe."

Chloe said, "Here, after the this part, 'I was finally old enough to go to the YMCA swimming class. I've wanted to go to the swimming class for years.'"

"Were you excited, scared? Is this a silly story?" I asked.

"No, I was nervous but a little excited."

"Okay, with your partners turn and talk about how you can help Chloe make her readers feel like they are right there."

Brandon suggested, "She could say, it was a humongous pool!"

Grace added on, saying, "She could say that it was cool and shivering cold."

"I could say it was long and deep like a mud pit and I hope I don't drown!" Chloe piped in.

"Good Job, writers! You inspired some ideas! You have a pen, right, Chloe? Add in what you want to say. Here are some Post-Its, because you don't have much space."

"Okay!" Chloe began writing her thoughts down quickly as the children and I helped other students also in need of feedback.

Notice how I vary the ways and times I encourage students to give feedback to each other. It is all too easy to teach students a few prompts, such as "I like the way you added details . . ." or "I think you can add more about . . ." and then leave it at that. Instead, I teach students to give the kind of specific feedback that I would give, and I provide many opportunities to practice doing so.

Learning to Write in Powerful Ways

Trying Out a Second Craft Move

ear Teachers,

In the first bend, you taught children ways to generate topics and get started writing their own personal narratives. The sessions in that bend were intended to help children develop the habits of writers: being observant, catching their thinking on paper, setting goals and using all they know to make their writing better. By the end of that bend, children will have written three to six personal narratives, and as in every unit of study, they will have taken the teaching of each day's minilesson and applied it either to their previous writing, making it even better, or to the new writing they are creating as they go forward.

Now, in Bend II of the unit, the goal has been to help children learn to use published texts to take their writing to the next level—you are teaching children how to study a text very very closely, learning from an author's techniques, and in this way, to take authors as mentors. The bend began with an invitation to children to think about their intentions as they compose, revise, develop, and experiment with their writing. "Writers try out different ways their stories could go," you will have said. "Writers decide to make their stories sad or interesting or full of awe . . ." Children then chose some ways their stories might go and began developing their writing accordingly.

Session 9, then, provided the resources children need to do that work: mentor texts. We describe how you might teach this bend using *Owl Moon*, but of course you could use any well-written text your class knows and you all love. You helped children through the process of carefully studying the powerful parts of the text, learning techniques to make the important parts of their own writing more powerful. In Session 9, you helped children name not only what was powerful about the writing, but also how the author made it that way. Now that you have that list of powerful parts of the text and the ways the author made them powerful, you are offering up, to the children, a way to transfer that learning to their own writing. They understand the power, they know how, and now they need practice!

What is key about this unit is the process of learning from texts, learning from close study, and then applying that learning to independent work. That is, the goal isn't just that children learn to describe what they see and hear in their texts, per se, or write comparisons (though of course, both of these craft moves can lead to powerful writing). Beyond this, you will want to teach them how to study a text they admire and use what they discover in any future writing project, as they see fit. To this end, it is important to give children repeated opportunities to practice applying what they've learned from a text again and again. In the last session, children took one observation from the chart and tried it out in their own writing. They will need to do this again (and perhaps again) to have the confidence and skill to take a book off the shelf and learn writing moves from it, on their own.

Welcome, then, to this session, which aims to lead children through doing just that. To create a session to help children move through this process, you can simply turn back to Session 10 and use the same architecture, the same kind of minilesson, this time swapping in a new author technique from the chart you made in Session 9 (see page 105).

In this letter, we use the example of making the reader hope or wonder with a character, but you can, of course, use any craft move your children have discovered that you think will raise the quality of their writing.

MINILESSON

Today's session aims to echo the one that precedes it so that children have a familiar format for studying and trying out a professional writer's craft moves. You won't, of course, begin with the miming game you initiated the day before, but you will emphasize that today is about trying to achieve another of Jane's effects, perhaps using some of her craft moves while also exploring new ways of achieving it. You will want to convey to your class that when you are learning something new, often it takes a great deal of practice. Practicing something that is hard or challenging can be invigorating work. You will want this work to seem challenging yet well worth trying! Instill in your kids the sense that they, too, can get better at writing, just like pianists and tennis players get better with practice. Today, this is the spotlight, practicing again how to use a craft move from a mentor author. You will want to select a new part in your class story to work on and find a part in Jane Yolen's text that does the same thing you want to do.

You might say something like, "Writers, today is all about practice and building up our writing muscles. Again, we're going to think back to the inquiry we did together the other day when we thought about how Jane wrote the powerful parts of *Owl Moon*. Yesterday, you studied how to try out craft moves in your writing. Remember how together we tried out how to make our readers feel like they were right there in our story about Goldie? Many of you stretched out the settings in your pieces. You added little details about what you saw and heard (or smelled or tasted or felt) all around you. Some of you wrote interesting comparisons that evoked even clearer images of your story's world. Put your thumb on your knee if you tried a craft move from *Owl Moon*—either a comparison, showing more about what you see and hear, or a different one."

Then, in your teaching point, you might say, "Today I want to teach you that trying out craft moves takes practice. I want to show you again how you can match a part in your own writing with a part in a book to write with more power."

Learning Writing Moves from Our Favorite Authors

WHAT is powerful?	WHY is it powerful?	HOW is it done?
Page 1 of <u>Owl Moon</u>	feels like you are there	names what character exactly: • sees • hears • feels makes a comparison
Right before owl arrives in <u>Owl Moon</u>, when the father calls out to it	you wonder what will happen next, and hope things turn out a certain way	• uses actions and images that show a character hopes for something • gives clues that something might happen • stretches out the story. The big thing doesn't happen right away.
showing the big idea in <u>Owl Moon</u> (pp. 11, 13, 29)	lets the reader know what is most important	uses repetition

During today's teaching, you will again demonstrate how to apply another of Jane Yolen's craft moves to your own writing. Here, you have a choice. You could demonstrate the second craft move we added to the chart in Session 10—how to make the reader wonder what will happen next, and hope things will turn out a certain way—or you could demonstrate a different craft move, based on what your class notices. We selected this one because it feels central to uncovering the power of *Owl Moon*, a book that is full of wonder and hope. And of course, learning how to write stories that make the reader wonder and hope alongside a character is a powerful technique to practice—whether a child is writing a piece about longing for a brother or trying to overcome a challenge, or making a goal or a new friend—that is, this craft move is transferable to many kinds of stories.

However, there are many other craft moves Jane has used that you could instead spotlight in this session. And, of course, the goal isn't so much that each and every child in the class tries out any particular craft move. Rather, the goal is that children think about the intended effect of a second craft move, and of possible ways to bring out the same in their own writing.

Tell your students that you are going to try a "Jane Yolen" to make your readers wonder and hope as they are reading your class story. In this example, we model how to add to the story about Goldie. You might say, "Watch while I add actions and images to our story that make readers wonder and hope with us."

In *Owl Moon*, the narrator isn't sure if the owl will, in fact, show up, and though she claims not to be "disappointed" when it at first doesn't appear, there is a sense throughout this book that she hopes it will. Little actions right before the owl appears—putting her mittens over her scarf and listening and looking so hard that her ears hurt and her eyes mist—get the reader hoping, too. Of course, you will have pointed this out a couple of days before. Today you'll quickly reiterate how this particular craft move works powerfully in Jane's book, how particular actions and images make the reader hope alongside the narrator, before trying out the same craft move in your writing.

Next, you'll demonstrate how you might borrow this "Jane Yolen" and apply it to the story you introduced in Session 10: "Writers, let's revisit my story about Goldie. We did some good work on it the other day, but I think now I can do even more by using this second 'Jane Yolen.' I bet I could get readers to wonder a little longer what's going on, and hope that Goldie's okay—before they find out she has died."

"First, let me remind myself how to do this craft move, I could add actions or images that show us hoping or wondering" (I held up one finger), "I could add little clues about what's going on" (I held up a second finger), "And I could stretch out this part so that the reader doesn't know right away that Goldie's dead."

"Here's my last version of that part," I said, pointing to the chart.

> We heard Tenzing crying. We all went to the fish tank. The room was filled with silence, just like before a storm. No one spoke.
>
> We saw our Goldie, floating on top of the water. She wasn't swimming. She was belly up in the tank. Her eyes were blank. They stared at nothing.

"I can *definitely* stretch out this part so that the reader wonders with us what's going on. Okay, here goes . . ." and I composed out loud while I wrote a new version on chart paper, tucking in commentary as I did, to unpack what I was doing:

> We heard Tenzing crying. We dropped everything and rushed to the fish tank (this action shows we are worried—and the reader will worry with us). The fish food was still in Tenzing's hand and her back was to the tank (That image of Tenzing with the food in her hand, back to the tank, builds even more wonder). The room was filled with silence, just like before a storm. No one spoke. The water was still. (Here's a little clue that something is wrong.)

"Where's Goldie?" Roccio asked.

Isabelle tapped the glass. "Come out, Goldie," she said. (These actions and words, too, show we are hoping to find our fish.)

Then Tenzing turned and pointed to something gold. (Notice how I've stretched out the story.)

We saw our Goldie, floating on top of the water. She wasn't swimming. She was belly up in the tank. Her eyes were blank. They stared at nothing.

Notice, here, that we added a bit of dialogue and then explained that people can say things in a story to make the reader wonder and hope. That was a choice we made because it felt natural to this story. You might decide that conveying yet another way to use this craft move will just overwhelm your class. If so, skip it.

You may also be wondering whether this teaching is any different than telling the story in itsy-bitsy steps, as children learned to do last year. Certainly, this work achieves a similar effect, and your students may realize this themselves. The angle here, however, is on inspiring wonder and hope in the reader—which adds sophistication to what children learned to do in first grade.

As in Session 9, for the active engagement, recruit children to help you further revise your story, trying out the same craft move in another part. In the case of the Goldie story, the class might work on the moment when we see Goldie belly up—or the part when we say goodbye. First, we'd reiterate what the craft move accomplishes so far. "Writers, the story has so many clues that Goldie is dead: the still water, that she is 'belly up' and her eyes are 'blank.' And now we *also* get the reader to hope by having Isabelle and Rocio do little things to find Goldie. So now what? Is there a new kind of wondering and hope we could add to the end of our story? Let's all try to remember what happened next."

With some prompting, the kids might recall that they had a big conversation about how to say goodbye to Goldie. Maybe the hope now is that she gets a proper send off. Kids could add in actions and words and images to show this new hope.

Your class story will, of course, differ from this one, but the work will be the same. You'll find parts of your story that can be stretched out with clues about the big thing that's about to happen, and with actions and images that help the reader hope alongside the characters. We suggest you think up various ways this might go in case your children need extra scaffolding during the active engagement.

After the minilesson, reiterate the various ways children have learned to make a reader wonder and hope: "Writers, there are many ways to get your reader to wonder and hope alongside your characters. If you think your story could use a little more of that feeling, you could try adding actions that show your character hoping, hoping, hoping, or you could drop little hints that make your reader wonder what will happen next. Or you could stretch out your story, so that the big part comes later." Then be sure to support children's independence. Recall the growing repertoire of craft moves the class has discovered, and tell children that what they decide to use in their work is their choice: "Writers, you might decide your story doesn't need to make the reader wonder or hope. Maybe your goal is to make your readers pay attention to something else—like a different strong emotion, or a beautiful image. Only you can decide what your story needs."

CONFERRING AND SMALL-GROUP WORK

By now, you have many things to balance during the workshop. Conferring and small-group work time will help you support students in multiple ways. First and foremost, you will want to teach children to write stories that are meaningful. Check to be sure that your students are writing with a strong sense of small moment and incorporating details such as step-by-step action, dialogue, and basic setting. Sometimes, when you teach craft moves, the actual sense of story can get lost, and students can forget to use all that they know about writing small moments. You may decide to pull some students for quick strategy lessons that address one or two of these areas.

Second, you will want to continue to ask kids, "What are you doing as a writer?" Expect a few different responses. Certainly, some kids may have intentions of what they want to show in their writing, but won't quite know how to do so. Others may be trying a craft move but won't be sure *why* they are using it. Both of these scenarios can lead to powerful conferring in which you help lift children's understanding not only of writing, but of how to study mentor texts.

Specifically, you will look at students' pieces and consider whose writing could use yet more suspense (or wondering and hope, as you've named it), and whose could use more details. Pull this group together to explicitly coach these writers how to stretch out their scenes like Jane Yolen does in *Owl Moon*. Remember, these are approximations. As you gather your students, have them bring not only their current piece of writing, but their entire folder. This way, if students "feel finished" with one piece, they can move right on to a second one—this time more independently. Second-grade writers need lots of practice. Having multiple pieces in their folders will not only set them up to approximate a strategy in their work, but will encourage them to apply what they are learning to many pieces.

As you did in Session 10, you may decide to pull the same or a different group of students to practice studying craft moves in *Owl Moon* via an inquiry. Discovering either new techniques or familiar ones in new places in the text is important work. This is important to do not only with the whole class, but also in one-on-one conferences and small groups, where you can either delve deeper with advanced students, or offer additional support to those who struggle. You may decide to bring out some of the insights this group has during today's mid-workshop or share. As you conduct this inquiry, have on hand your piece of shared writing to refer to as the group names what the mentor author does. You can "test out" what the group notices on this piece, to see if the group has discovered something transferable. At the end of the group work, these students can turn back to their own writing, to see if they can try some of the same things they just discovered.

MID-WORKSHOP TEACHING

After working with one of the small groups described above, pause students. Remind them of some of the things they have been studying over the past few days, and stress that it is important to be mindful not just of *what* craft moves to use, but also *where* and *why*. Some of your students will have tried one move, one time, in one place in their writing. Share that writers like Jane Yolen usually don't just do one thing, one time, in one place. Instead, they use a few writing moves throughout a piece of writing, and in many different stories.

You can show how on both page 3 and page 7 of *Owl Moon*, Jane uses comparisons, just like the class discovered she did on page 2. Cite the example of one of your students from a conference or a small group who tried to make the reader wonder what was going to happen next in a few places in one story, or in a few different stories. You might read these aloud so that the class hears another example of what this craft move sounds like in one of their peers' writing, or just hold up the work. Then ask students to look over their own pieces to notice what they tried. Have them put a Post-it on that part and think, "Should I try that move somewhere else in my piece or in another story?" They could then mark two or three more places in their writing to develop further in the next workshop. This not only sets children up to transfer what they are learning to multiple parts or pieces, and to revise, it also supports them to make a concrete plan for their work.

SHARE

Again, you will echo Session 10 by referring to two new student pieces in this share session. Follow the same protocol of teaching students how to contribute ideas to another student's work. Consider selecting students who chose a place in their writing where they could use support making readers wonder more, or hope for something alongside the character. Have the first student name what she tried as a writer. You may need to reread the section that comes right before—or ask her to share it. Then, have students turn and talk about what they would add. Remember, the class is not writing this piece; rather, children are giving the writer suggestions about how one part could go. Write down the examples students offer on an acetate, so as to not disturb the student's writing. Then, share out a few suggestions with the whole group and ask the writer to think about these as she decides what and how to revise. Give the writing back to the student to revise, while moving on to a second student writer to repeat the process. Use your chart to point out to the class that there are multiple ways for writers to do this work. Try to keep the process as open as possible, allowing students to approximate the work, rather than to do it perfectly, or to try out ways you might not have even considered.

Working on a shared text gives students practice using a skill while receiving the support of fellow writers. You are not reteaching the same skill; instead, you are coaching kids with the next stage of the process—actually implementing the work across their writing. This is valuable work, designed to deepen students' understanding of the craft moves they are learning, and to hone their ability to transfer these more seamlessly to their own writing.

Enjoy,

Julia and Amanda

Emulating Authors in Ways that Matter

Revising in Meaningful Ways

O FTEN ONE MINILESSON IS A CORRECTION—or a fine-tuning—of another. We teach children ellipses—and we then teach how to keep ellipses from swamping their pieces. This minilesson serves this purpose. When you first invite children to emulate craft moves in books, often they will try out those moves in seemingly bizarre places, or without any real intention, missing the crucial component of *why* an author might choose to use a particular craft move in her writing. That is, they can add comparisons, details that describe what their character sees, hears, and feels (and even a feeling of suspense), without any clear understanding of how these craft moves will improve their writing—and so the end result is that their writing *isn't* improved.

Today, then, you'll nudge your students to look beyond *what* craft moves they have learned from the mentor text in order to think about what the moves accomplish. That is, you'll look more closely at the *Why* on your class chart. You may be thinking that you have already gone over the "why" with students in the previous two sessions, but if you are finding—as we have found when piloting this unit—that your students are not yet adding craft moves to their writing in meaningful ways, then explicit teaching and demonstration are needed. You cannot expect your students to learn by osmosis. To improve as writers, they need crystal clear feedback and concrete steps to take when thinking about how—and *why*—to include a technique they have learned from a mentor author.

In this session, you'll demonstrate for kids what a haphazard addition of a new kind of craft move can look like, and then you'll ask them to join you in making a meaningful, revision to your writing. You'll revisit the notion of writing with intent and invite children to revise their own writing with an eye on meaning.

IN THIS SESSION, you'll teach students that when writers study mentor authors they think not only *what* this author has done that they could try out but *why* this author has done this. Then they revise to make sure that they've emulated craft moves in ways that make sense.

GETTING READY

- ✔ *Owl Moon* by Jane Yolen, or another mentor text, for you (see Teaching) and one copy for each student (see Share)

- ✔ Your own writing, enlarged for students to see (see Teaching)

- ✔ Post-it notes (see Share)

- ✔ Chart paper, markers (see Share)

- ✔ "Language Choices Jane Yolen Made" chart (see Share)

Emulating Authors in Ways that Matter
Revising in Meaningful Ways

CONNECTION

Tell children that sometimes we forget *why* we are doing something new.

"Writers, you know how when you want something, like a bike, or a new toy, or a video game, suddenly everywhere you look, you see that thing? Last year, I wanted to buy a car, but I wasn't sure what kind. My friend said, 'Buy a hybrid!' All of a sudden, do you know what happened? All I saw were hybrids on the road! Hundreds of them! It was as if they were the only cars on the road, that's how many of them I noticed.

"Now that we have studied a few parts of Jane's book, *Owl Moon*, it's the same thing for all of us. We are seeing possible craft moves everywhere we look! But here's the thing, writers. When people learn to do something new—sometimes we do that thing again and again, as often as we can, and in the process, we lose sight of *why* we're doing it."

❧ **Name the teaching point.**

"So today, I want to talk to you again about intent. Specifically, I want to teach you that when writers revise, they study mentor authors, thinking not only, '*What* has this author done that I could try out?' but also '*Why* has this author done this?' Then they look at their own writing to be sure that they've emulated craft moves in ways that make sense—in ways that make their stories better."

TEACHING

Demonstrate the process you use to think about *why* the mentor author writes as she does.

"Let me show you what I mean. One of the things we've studied together in Jane's writing is her use of comparisons. Jane uses comparisons so beautifully. Let's look again at a few." I read aloud:

Somewhere behind us a train whistle blew, long and low, like a sad sad song.

This analogy brings home the importance of teaching students to read with a writer's consciousness. It's true that once a person's consciousness changes, everything changes. That probably happened to you when you began teaching. Suddenly, everything you did became grist for your teaching mill. You'd be at a concert and think, "I should bring my students to a concert. Does this symphony have special programs for kids?" If your teaching has gone well so far, some of your children will see writing lessons in texts all around them.

I paused, letting the line fill the room, then I read:

And when their voices faded away it was as quiet as a dream.

"So if I'm going to learn from Jane in a purposeful way, I'd not only notice a powerful part and name what she did, I'd also ask myself why. *Why* does she use comparisons? What is the main thing she wants to get across to the reader?

"Hmm, . . . It seems to me that Jane wants to show us how very still this journey into the woods at night is. She wants us to feel, with the narrator, the quiet all around. Remember how she tells us, 'If you go owling you have to be quiet'? They are both quiet, and so are the woods. And we are too. It's almost like we're holding our breath, following the path, on the lookout for that owl. I think Jane wants us to feel like we're there, so she uses comparisons that paint a picture, pulling us into this still night in the woods."

Share a piece of writing in which the craft move you tried does not bring out the story's meaning.

"Yesterday, I came across a comparison I'd made, under Jane's influence. At first, I was kind of proud of myself. But when I reread, something didn't feel quite right. Listen to the beginning and see what you think. You can also follow along with your eyes." I put my entry on the overhead so children could see:

"Hurry up!" Frances said. I was standing on the ocean shore. My bathing suit was as red as a tomato. I was scared. "Come on!" she said, and swam out farther.

"Are you noticing what I noticed when I reread? I made a comparison, just like Jane did, but it doesn't really do anything to bring out my story's meaning. It's almost as if I made any ol' comparison, not a *meaningful* one."

Demonstrate revising your writing by using a craft technique in a way that enhances meaning.

"Let me look at my story again and think, 'What do I *really* want to get across to my reader? How do I *really* want my reader to feel?' What I really want my readers to know is how terrified I felt just looking at those waves. The color of my bathing suit—or that it looks like a tomato—is beside the point. So that comparison doesn't push forward my story's meaning. If I want to show how scared I was, I need to make a comparison that shows that. Hmm, . . . How about if I talk about the *waves*, not my bathing suit?

"They were awfully tall and foamy, those waves. That's what made them so scary. They were even bigger than Jane's 'giant statue' trees! How about this: 'The waves towered above me, like steep, snow-capped mountains.' That works. Who wouldn't be terrified of a mountain-sized wave?

"I'll add that in. Listen to this new version, and see if you think this comparison works better to bring out my story's meaning:

What a beautiful text this is! Read it well, and read it often. The book is chock-full of images that paint a picture for the reader, drawing us in. You will, of course, want to read aloud parts that you and your particular class of children noticed earlier, using those to model whatever craft move you intend to illustrate in this session.

When I'm trying to teach something fairly complicated to very young children, I make sure my examples aren't subtle in the least. Most little kids will be able to pick up that my description of my bathing suit leaves something to be desired.

> "Hurry up!" Frances said. I was standing on the ocean shore. I was scared. The waves towered above me, like steep, snow-capped mountains. "Come on!" she said, and swam out farther.

"Thumbs up if that comparison works better than the one about the tomato-colored bathing suit."

The class gave me an enthusiastic thumbs up.

"Do you see how I pulled back to think about how a craft move I tried didn't work, and then revised it so that it did? That's the kind of revision work that writers do when they want to make a piece better, or on the go, as they're drafting."

ACTIVE ENGAGEMENT

Ask the class to help you revise your text, again using the same craft move to convey your meaning.

"I think I might add one more comparison, but I want to be sure I do so in a way that shows how I felt when I went into the water. Listen as I read the rest of my story. I'd love your help."

> "Hurry up!" Frances said. I was standing on the ocean shore. I was scared. The waves towered above me, like steep, snow-capped mountains. "Come on!" she said, and swam out farther.
>
> I dipped my toe in and quickly pulled it back out. Then, before I changed my mind, I ran into the water and swam to her.
>
> We jumped wave after wave. "This isn't so bad," I thought.
>
> All of a sudden, I saw a big wave coming. The wave came closer and closer. "You gotta dive into this one. Go under," Frances said.
>
> I called out to Frances, but it was too loud for her to hear. I did a little half dive. Then the wave tumbled me down, down, down.

"Hmm, . . . I wonder if I could add comparisons to other parts to show how scared I was. Can you help? Turn and talk to your partner."

As children talked, I called out little tips: "Remember, a comparison could take different forms. In addition to what I see, I could add something about what I hear, or taste, or feel." After a couple minutes, I called on a few kids.

"You could add to the part when you're about to go under," Lindsay said. "You could compare the noise of the wave to something really scary and loud."

"Aha. So what might that be?"

It would be easy to forgive the fact that reading-writing connections for second-graders result in craft choices that don't improve the quality of a text—but I believe in being direct and ambitious. There's not much risk in going for the gold!

This is a great idea. The only reason I was able to elicit this wonderful example is that I listened in while children talked and heard a few especially powerful suggestions. I also interacted with them, eliciting a bit more detail so that by the time I called on these children, they were ready!

"A lion!" her partner, Stephen, called out.

"A lion. So the waves *sounded* like a lion?" I asked.

"The waves *roared* like a lion!" several kids called out.

"Great suggestion. Listen to that part now."

> All of a sudden, I saw a big wave coming. The wave came closer and closer. It roared in my ears, like a lion.

LINK

Sum up for the children what they need to do in their own writing to apply what they have learned from other authors and to make their writing better.

"This is not easy work, writers. But I think you can do it. Right now, will you pick a piece of writing to revise in similar ways? Some of you may already have one in mind; others of you may want to leaf through your folders, like I did. Try to find a piece that could use some fixing up. You can follow these steps.

"Go back and study where your author used a technique that you've used. Look really closely and think, '*Why* did the author do it this way?' Try to get some ideas in your head.

"Then, look again at your work. Think, 'I could do this *even better*.' On a new sticky note, write a new try on top of the old one. Make sure your revisions make your writing better. Ask yourself, 'Does this revision make my reader feel the way I hope she feels? Does it bring out my story's meaning?'

"Writers, today I noticed a *comparison* that didn't bring out my story's meaning, and I tried adding different comparisons that *would* help. But I could have also thought about other things, like the lines of dialogue in my story, the actions, my word choice. Writers revise for all sorts of things, paying attention to how their craft moves make their writing better—or not. So today, as you write and revise, be on the lookout for the different kinds of things you might revise in your writing."

These are complex and multifaceted directions. I know, as I say them, that some children will be able to follow them, and others will need a lot of support.

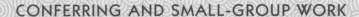

Helping Students Increase the Volume of Their Writing

IF YOU HAVE SPENT A FEW DAYS FOCUSING on craft moves, you will want to check in and make sure that students are writing with volume, writing many stories, and using what they know about the qualities of good storytelling as they write. Before the workshop starts, I often try and steal a little time to quickly study students' folders. Sometimes I collect five at a time to see what kind of work is happening. I might pick one thing to notice, like volume, or spelling, or elaboration. As I study their pieces, I look for patterns. I either turn these patterns into teaching points for minilessons or use them to decide upon various types of small groups to pull. As I studied Amara's folder, I saw she had one piece (Figure 12–1) that was one page long, only four sentences, that she had been working on for three days.

So I thought to myself, "What is going on here? How is Amara spending her writing time? Have I not conferred with her enough? Is something getting in her way?" I decided to ask her.

I pulled a chair up alongside hers and said, "Amara, what is going on? I notice you have been on the same page for three days. How can I help you?"

"I don't know." She smiled and then shrugged.

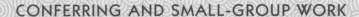

FIG. 12–1 The first page of Amara's writing lacks volume given it has been worked on for three days.

> ## MID-WORKSHOP TEACHING
> ### Writers Try Out Craft Moves in Many Parts of Many Pieces
>
> "Writers, can I stop you for a second? I am going to press 'pause' in your writing," I called out from the middle of the room. I waited for students' attention. "I see that some of you are still on the same story. Make sure you're not belaboring just one craft move in one part. You should be aiming to try out more purposeful craft moves in lots of parts of multiple pieces. And yes, earlier I said you might want to revisit an old story, but you may also want to start new pieces, too. You should have around six to seven long stories in your folder. Some of you might have a few more that are shorter. You can try out what you learned today in both old pieces and new ones. In new pieces, you will be doing on-the-go revision, adding purposeful craft moves as you draft.
>
> "Right now, look at your work and say to yourself, 'What do I need to do as writer? Do I need to start a new piece or continue adding into an older one?' If you are adding, remember, don't just add a little here and there—make sure you are trying out different things in lots of parts! If you need to, start a new piece! Okay, I'm pushing 'play' now—continue your writing."

"Well, Amara, if you look at Grace's stories, and Mohammed's and April's, they are all writing lots of pages and they write down the page, too!"

She told me she didn't know why she couldn't move on. I pointed out all the things I could see she had tried and asked what was going to happen next. Amara shrugged again. I made a silly drawing of a goal post in the margin of her book, told her she had nine minutes to write to that goal post, and then I'd be back to see how her writing had progressed. As I got up to leave, Amara dove into writing.

"Wait, I don't even get to say, 'Go'?" I asked. Amara giggled. "Go! Write! Good luck! I don't know if you can do it. It's a tall order," I dared.

Seven minutes later I circled back and reminded her there were just two minutes left.

"But, look, I'm done!" She held her writing up to show me (Figure 12–2).

"Are you on to the next? Did you set another goal?" She shook her head. "Do it! I'll be back in another ten." After about five minutes she shouted from across the room, "I did it!"

"Do it again," I called back. Amara continued to work furiously, clearly reenergized by the challenge of writing toward a goal.

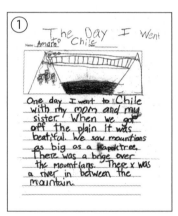

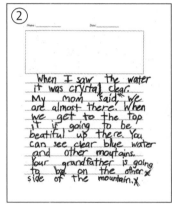

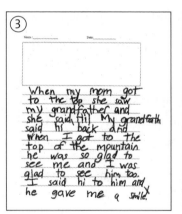

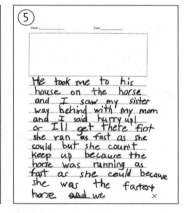

One day I went to Chile with my mom and my sister. When we got off the plane it was beautiful. We saw mountains as big as a Kapok tree. There was a bridge over the mountains. There was river in between the mountains.

When I saw the water it was crystal clear. My mom said, "We are almost there. When we get to the top it is going to be beautiful up there. You can see clear blue water and other mountains. Your grandfather is going to be on the other side of the mountain.

When my mom got to the top she saw my grandfather and she said, "Hi" My grandfather said hi back ad when I got to the top of the mountain he was so glad to see me and I was glad to see him too. I said hi to him and he gave me a smile.

My sister said nothing but he still smiled. I asked him if he had a horse for me to ride and he said, "yes." SO I went down the mountain to see the horse. When I got down I saw a beautiful horse waiting for me. The horses name was Vivaracha. I was happy to see her and she was happy to see me.

He took me to his house on the horse and I saw my sister way behind with my mom and I said, "Hurry up! or I'll get there first." She ran as fast as she could but she couldn't keep up because the horse was running as fast as she could because she was the fastest horse.

FIG. 12–2 Amara's revised writing that she accomplished by setting volume goals (making X marks on the page)

Noticing the Words Mentor Authors Choose

Ask students to reread *Owl Moon*, this time with a lens toward noticing editing moves.

"Writers, earlier I talked to you about your new writer's eyes—how you're seeing possible craft moves everywhere you look. We're going to shift a bit now. We're going to look at the craft moves that relate especially to word choices. Authors choose words that are as exact and clear and meaningful as they can be. In just a few days, we are going to be celebrating your best writing, so you will want to revise it for meaning *and* edit it.

"Right now, with your writing circle (remember the foursome you were a part of the other day?) you are going to quickly reread *Owl Moon*, and this time you will look at the exact words Jane uses and the little things she has done. You might notice how lines of text sound, or words that are particularly precise or beautiful. Use a Post-it to mark the line or two that jump out at you as especially effective."

Have students share their observations about what is happening at the word level of the text.

After a few minutes, I called out, "Now share what you've noticed with your writing circle. Try to talk in specific ways about what you saw." As children did this work, I circled the room, listening in. Then I reconvened the group.

"Writers, when I gesture to you, read one word or line or sentence you marked and say why it works so well."

I pointed to Alex, who read, "Our feet crunched over the crisp snow . . . " I gestured for him to explain, and he added, "I like the way it sounds. The crunching. And the crisp snow."

"Yes, it's almost as if you can hear that snow. And *crunched—crisp*—see how they begin the same way? That's called *alliteration*. Writers use alliteration to make their writing musical." I added this to our chart and gestured to Stephen.

"I like how she repeats words. *Or* and *off.*"

You'll need to figure out a way to put a bit of the text into your kids' hands. Some teachers duplicate a page or two, distributing that to kids, or they type up a transcript. Some copy a page or two onto chart paper or use technology to enlarge the text.

"I've got two parts," he said, and read:

> *or about the woods*
> *or the moon*
> *or the cold*

Then,

> *off the scarf*
> *off my mouth*

"Great observation, Stephen! She's almost listing. Hmm, . . . It's like she's drawing our attention to that part by repeating those words."

I pointed to Justin, who said, "A farm dog answered the train." "That's funny. Dogs don't talk!"

"They don't, do they? Jane could have written, 'A farm dog barked,' but she decided to have the dog 'answer' the train. Isn't that an interesting word choice? It's almost like the dog and train are having a conversation, like people. Writers call that *personification*, when something that isn't a person is described like it is a person. "One line I especially loved is this one: 'an echo came threading its way through the trees.' That threading echo is a bit like the answering dog. In my head I see a needle and thread, moving through the trees, as if it is weaving. But it is the echo—not thread! What an image! It's as if Jane thought to herself, 'What exactly do I want to say here that will sound beautiful and say what I mean?' I'm realizing that Jane doesn't use just any words. She uses exact, beautiful words. I'll add that to our list."

"Writers, I heard so many more interesting observations. We don't have time to share any more right now, but I encourage all of you to share what you noticed with one another."

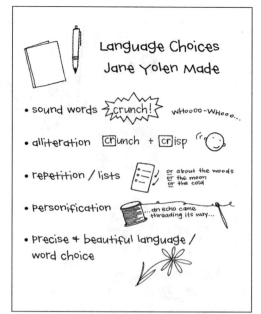

The Perfect Day

read it!

Rocks

read it!

By: Tenzin

Best!

① Name: Tenzin C   Date: ____

We're finally going to Canada!" I yelled scred. My heart was pounding so fast! Boom! Boom! I was in my room. I heard some cars honking. Beep! I ran to the window to see who was making all the beeping sound. I looked down but I didn't see anything. The car left. I thought

② Name: _____   Date: _____

We went outside. My dad said, "You could say bye to every one of your friends." I said, "Okay." We went to the next building. I said bye to everyone I knew. But "Bye" I whisperd to my friend.

③ Name: _____   Date: _____

Tenzin

We walked to the train. I was feeling so exhausted. We finally got there. I was so droopy. I was even more droopy when we were waiting for the train. When the train came. I was so relieved.

④ Name: _____   Date: _____

We got on a bus. My mom told me to order food, but I was too scared. So my mom said she'll come. I felt a little better. My stumache was grumbling. When we got there, My legs were shaking. I said, "C-c-can we have lunch?" I said in a quite voice. "Yes ma'am" said the man. I was so proud of myself.

FIG. 12–3   Tenzing uses specific language and words to capture her moment of going to Canada.

Mining Mentor Texts for Word Choice

Studying and Revising for Precise and Specific Language

IN THE PREVIOUS SESSION, you set children up to consider craft through the lens of revision. You suggested that revising in thoughtful ways means thinking not only, "*What* did this author do that I might try?" but "*Why* has the author done this?" and then reviewing one's own work to be sure that the craft moves selected have been used thoughtfully—that they make a piece of writing stronger and convey one's intended meaning.

Today, you will again ask children to look closely at their writing, now through the lens of word choice. During the previous share, children selected lines in *Owl Moon* that particularly stood out as effective language moves. When we've taught these minilessons, children have noticed lines whose words had a particular sound (alliteration), repeating (list-like) lines, parts with comparisons or that created particular images, or lines in which dogs and shadows acted like people (personification). Your students may pay attention to other things. Perhaps they'll focus more on line breaks or on echoes. It is always fun to see what things jump out to each group of kids. Of course, if you are hoping that your students notice something in particular, you can always draw their attention to that thing during the demonstration part of this lesson.

In today's combined teaching and active engagement, you'll work together as a class to notice ways to revise one of your stories (we selected the one we used in the previous demonstration) to make it more precise and powerful. As part of this, you'll point out a place in which a detail does *not* work to enhance your piece, and will then show how to revise that part so that it makes your piece stronger. In this way, today's session builds on the work the class did in the last session. During this part of the lesson, you might focus on whatever you think your children most need help with in their own writing. We chose dialogue tags and strong, precise language, but you could focus on adding poetic language, or on varying the lengths of sentences, or on making positioning phrases in purposeful ways, or on using words that create a clearer image. There are countless options for the sorts of revision moves to spotlight. Let your particular students' needs and your own teaching interests act as guides.

IN THIS SESSION, you'll teach students that writers edit not only for standard conventions but also for the way their writing sounds. They can use mentor authors to learn about precise, beautiful language.

GETTING READY

✔ Student writing folders (see Connection)

✔ Your own writing, enlarged for students to see (see Teaching and Active Engagement)

✔ Student copies of the text of *Owl Moon*, marked from the previous day's Share session (see Teaching and Active Engagement)

✔ Student writing folders (see Share)

Mining Mentor Texts for Word Choice

Studying and Revising for Precise and Powerful Language

CONNECTION

Ask students to reread the writing that is in their folder, selecting two pieces for the upcoming mini-celebration.

For today's workshop, I asked students to bring their writing folders to the meeting area. "Writers, I have some super exciting news for you! Tomorrow, is our first writing celebration of second grade! You will be sharing your writing with readers!"

"At this point, I bet your folders are chock-full of writing. Am I right? What you're going to do right now is choose just two pieces you want to publish. To pick those pieces, there are a couple of questions you can ask yourself. One, 'Is this a piece of writing I really care about and want others to read?' And two, 'Did I include a few Jane Yolens in my writing?' Don't worry if your piece isn't perfect or the best writing you've ever done, or even if it's not finished yet. You'll have some time today to fix it up before our celebration tomorrow. Got it? Right now, take some time to read through the writing on both sides of your folder. I'll come around to help if you're having trouble choosing."

As students sorted through the writing in their folders, I circulated among them, answering questions and providing coaching and support for those who needed it. Once students had selected their pieces, I said, "We've been spending a lot of time looking at *Owl Moon*, learning lots of strategies to improve parts of our writing. But we can also use mentor texts to think about specific word devices, too."

❖ **Name the teaching point.**

"Today I want to teach you that writers don't just revise whole parts of their writing. They also revise for the way their writing sounds. You can use mentor authors to learn how to make careful and thoughtful word choices that capture the sound and beauty of your writing when you revise."

Throughout this series, there are times when the connection sets children up to be ready to learn from the minilesson. Sometimes, for example, it is in the connection that children generate a topic for writing. When that work is done before the rest of the minilesson, it means that as writers listen to the teaching, they can apply it to their topic. Today's connection accomplishes a similar goal. By giving children a minute or two to select the pieces they'll publish, I set them up to listen with an ear for how the instruction relates to their specific feats.

TEACHING AND ACTIVE ENGAGEMENT

Conduct a "symphony share," where each student shares out examples of beautiful language he or she noticed in *Owl Moon*. Point out how Jane has made some important choices about language and how they can do the same.

"Writers, during our share yesterday, lots of you realized that Jane uses precise and beautiful language throughout *Owl Moon*. You kept coming up to me or to one another, reading lines. Let's share those now. Please open your folders and take out your copies of *Owl Moon*. When I point to you, just read the line you noticed." I pointed to each child as if conducting an orchestra.

One by one, children read their lines aloud:

> *"It was as quiet as a dream."*
> *". . . as if reading a map up there"*
> *"The moon made his face into a silver mask."*
> *"The shadow hooted again."*
> *"They stained the white snow."*
> *"The snow below it was whiter than the milk in a cereal bowl."*
> *"the kind of hope that flies on silent wings under a shining Owl Moon"*

"You have studied how Jane Yolen uses precise and specific words in *Owl Moon*. Not only does she create a beautiful *sound* in her writing (almost like music), she also shows her reader exactly what the characters saw, heard, and felt. This is something she does throughout her story, in every part. You can do this in your writing, too.

"Now that we are getting ready to publish, it's time to revise a bit more. You can look to Jane, and other mentor authors, to help you make precise language choices. Now that you've studied and noticed the beautiful, precise language that Jane uses in her writing, you can do the same in your own writing."

Read your story to the class and model reflecting on the language choices you have made.

"Watch how I try this with my story about going into the ocean. I'm going to read the beginning of my story and think, 'Where can I add more beautiful language or change some of my words to be more precise?' Then I'll see what I could borrow from Jane Yolen to help me. I might be able to make a comparison like she did, or say what I did and how I did it, or I could even make an alliteration. Will you also be on the lookout for what you think I can do to this story as I revise?"

> *"Hurry up!" Frances said. I was standing on the shore. I was scared. The waves towered above me, like steep, snow-capped mountains. "Come on!" she said, and swam out farther.*

Once children have learned how to do a symphony share, this becomes a ritual you can rely on easily, with no fuss and bother. It is a quick way to get their voices and ideas in the minilesson.

"Are you all getting ideas? I see some thumbs. See if this matches what you were thinking. The comparison I wrote about the waves is precise, but I can make my story even more specific." I reread the first sentence. "Well, Frances did say 'hurry up' to me. But if I wanted to use a word or a couple of words to show *how* she spoke, I could say, 'Frances said nicely' or 'Frances said urgently,' or 'Frances 'called.' Yeah, she didn't just *say* it, she said it *loudly*! I'll change 'said' to 'called.' Were you thinking the same thing?" I pointed to Ramon. He nodded. "That is something Jane does often in her own story. She includes not just *what* people say, but *how* they say it. I am going to do it, too!" I edited my writing while the students looked on.

"Let me look at the next sentence. 'I was standing on the ocean's shore.' How could I make this sound more beautiful or more precise, like *Owl Moon*? I could say, 'I was standing still on the shore.' Ooh! An alliteration: standing still! I like that sound. And the stillness suggests that I'm not eager to go into the water (I wasn't!)."

Give students an opportunity to revise your writing.

"Will you *all* help with this next part? Let's make it also sound precise and more beautiful." I began to read.

> "Hurry up!" Frances called. I was standing still on the ocean's shore. The waves towered above me, like steep, snow-capped mountains. "Come on!" she said, and swam out farther.

"In this first part I made an alliteration *and* a comparison! What about the next sentence? ('Come on,' she said, and swam out farther.) Can you help? Turn and talk to your partner about how you could make it more precise."

After a bit, I shared out some findings and added a few. "I heard Lindsay say that I could change 'said' to 'shouted'! That is definitely more specific. Frances was really excited. She couldn't tell how scared I was. Stephen suggested I add, 'farther out into the deep dark water.' What a great image; that makes the ocean seem even scarier! Hold onto your other ideas for now and let's reread what we have so far!"

> "Hurry up!" Frances called. I was standing still on the ocean's shore. The waves looked like steep, snow-capped mountains. "Come on!" she shouted, and swam out farther into the deep dark water.

You may decide to practice this work on another part of your story, to give your students extra support, or you might want to see if they can transfer the work to another story—perhaps the one about the shared class experience. Or, if your students now have a clear sense of how this editing work goes, you might channel them to edit their own writing. Make sure your decision responds to the needs of your class.

LINK

Send students off, reminding them to use both the craft strategies and the language choices they've learned from _Owl Moon_ to get their writing ready for the celebration.

"Writers, it's time to get your pieces ready for tomorrow's celebration. You can revise or edit your stories, using all that you have learned. Isn't it amazing how just one book, just one writer, can teach us so much? You have some hard work ahead of you to get those stories into good shape! Are you up for the challenge?

"When you are working today, if you do something in your writing to make your words precise or beautiful, will you circle it or place a star next to it so that I see what you are trying? I'm going to stop our workshop about halfway through so that you can quickly share with your neighbor what you have been trying. Off you go!"

Planning and Reflecting on Your Conferences and Small-Group Teaching

YOU WILL LIKELY WANT to lead one or two spontaneous small-group lessons today, and after. Lead this sort of small-group work if, midway into a conference, you realize that other students would benefit from the work you intend to do with the one writer. Look at your conference notes to see who else could use similar support. Then, pull those students alongside the original child. Of course, another way to form a small group is to just gather a few writers who need similar support from the start.

Today, I pulled a small group consisting of Mohammed, Chloe, and Anna—three writers who seemed reluctant to revise their pieces. I asked them to bring their writing folders with them to the rug. Once they'd convened, I suggested they each look back over *Owl Moon*, noticing the precise language they had admired previously. I then suggested they turn to their own writing, and work on including more precise, beautiful language.

Notice that the early rallying cry at the start of this small group was brief. I mostly wanted to get children started on the revision work they had resisted, that I now planned to support. My goal was to spend most of the small-group time coaching kids to think about their own pieces. To coach each of them several times, my coaching needed to be lean and quick. In the first five minutes, Chloe was writing up a storm. I decided to send her back to her table. Meanwhile, I kept Mohammed and Anna in the group, and continued coaching them. After about ten minutes, I sent them back to their writing spots to continue this work. I then reflected on whether any of them could use a second day of coaching. Should I provide less or more scaffolding?

MID-WORKSHOP TEACHING
Using Writing Partners as Editing Partners

"Writers, remember I said that I was going to give you time to share with a neighbor some of the edits that you have been trying out in your work. I asked you to star or circle moves that you are trying or worked on. If you haven't yet done that, do it now. Then share with your neighbor what you tried and why. Neighbors, please be listening and ready to give a tip to help your friend use more precise language, make the reader wonder, or bring the reader right into the story.

"If you only have *one* place in your writing that you edited using Jane Yolen moves, make sure you find other parts as well. Name those parts with your neighbor! Then keep writing. If you need extra support with *how* to edit using a craft move, ask your partner for some conferring time in the partner area."

After each small group, I take time to reflect on and redesign and configure my small groups. I want to be sure that they are fluid and flexible, and that they carry students across time, through a series of teachings that can help them incorporate a new goal into their repertoire.

Here are the first two pages Mohammed worked on revising (see Figure 13–1):

On one nightly night there was the moon so bright and I was going to a party. It got really dark. But no problem. I got my best clothes that I could find. Then we walked 3 blocks. The cold whistle of the wind was blowing as if a windy place with a ghost town because nobody was outside. After we went in the warm nice car it was much more warm. When we came to the party, it was so big and there was a lot of people. The people looked like busy bees going all over the place. It sounded like a big person was talking on a microphone. Then when I went closer, I saw my friend. And he was happy to see me. He said, "Do you want to play?" I said, "We can't." He said, "Why not?" I said, "The guards said we can't play until everybody goes home. They said if you go in you can't go outside. Because it is too cold." He said, "But we could play a little." So we played tag. We ran and ran in circles 3 times. And then we got tired. We just sat down.

As you move on in your workshop, you will want to reflect on the general patterns of your student work. Can you tell that the writing is improving across the weeks? Are your students' understandings about writing also growing and deepening? These questions are critical to study and answer. You want to see not only your most struggling writer improving, but also your strongest writer making strides to deepen his or her writing knowledge base.

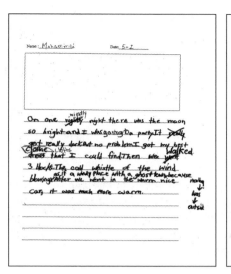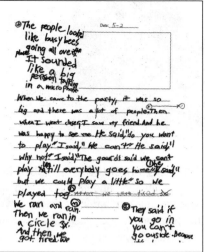

FIG. 13–1 First two pages Mohammed worked on revising

Interviewing Writing Partners Can Teach Both Partners about Writing

" WRITERS, I THOUGHT THIS WOULD BE a great opportunity to talk with your partners about what you are doing as writers. Here's yet another great thing about partners. When you talk to yours about his or her writing, often you get ideas for your *own* writing. Sometimes you'll find yourself inspired by your partner's ideas; you'll learn ways that he or she is working that can help *you* as you work, too. Just as you've been studying Jane Yolen, so too, you can study each other! You can be writing teachers to one another!"

I pointed to one partnership and said, "Rocio, you can teach Alex! And then Alex, you can teach Rocio!" Then I pointed to another partnership and said, "Justin, you can teach Isabelle! And then, Isabelle, you can teach Justin!" The kids smiled.

"So, let's try it. Alex, come on up here, for just a minute. Bring your writing folder." I patted a chair I'd pulled next to mine and he joined me in the hot spot.

Addressing the class, I said, "I've been struggling to come up with ideas lately, so I'm going to ask Alex how he came up with ideas for *his* story."

Then I turned to Alex and said, "So, Alex, can you help me out a little?" He nodded.

"Okay, the rest of you, listen closely. You may get ideas, too!" I said, then turned to Alex. "So Alex, what's your current story about?"

"It's about this time when my dad took me to the zoo."

"Okay. So tell us, how exactly did you come up with that story idea? Why did you pick that topic?"

"Well, I started thinking about times I've been with my dad alone, which isn't really that often, because I have two brothers and a sister. And then I remembered this time after the dentist when my dad took me to the zoo. And we saw a tiger. It was cool."

Before Alex could share details of the tiger, I said, "Ah, so you thought about something that doesn't happen very often that's special to you—spending time with your dad."

"Yeah," Alex said. "It was me and him only."

"You know, this is giving me an idea. I have a really dear friend who lives 3,000 miles away, on the other side of the country. I rarely see her—so times when she visits me or I visit her stick out in the same way. I bet I could write a story about one of those visits."

I turned to the class and said, "Writers, do you see how interviewing Alex about how he came up with his idea got me to think about stories I could write?

"Each one of you has a teacher in one another—so you can get ideas from lots of different writers.

"Right now, turn and interview your partner in the same way. Find out how he or she got an idea. You might go further, too. You might ask, "How did that moment make you feel?" or "What was the most important part, and how did you revise to show that?"

Rereading and Quick Editing
Preparing for a Mini-Celebration

ear Teachers,

It's the final day of your second bend and you will want to celebrate the work your second-graders have done so far! Your children have been doing double duty as readers and writers in this single unit, examining *Owl Moon* with a magnifying glass and then switching gears to try out the craft moves they notice in their own writing. This is sophisticated, heady work, and you'll want to make a big deal of what your kids have accomplished.

In the previous session, you asked children to pick several pieces to edit and fancy up in preparation for today's mini-celebration, and children practiced interviewing one child about his writing process. Today, you'll give everyone in the class a chance to talk about what they have tried out and to share a few favorite parts of their writing.

Today's minilesson, then, will be all about editing and fancying up the pieces children picked in the previous session. Young writers often rush through the editing part of writing, believing that the real work lies in writing. But the difference between a piece that impresses its author and one that impresses an audience often lies in the placement of a comma, the space between two lines of text, the spelling of a word.

MINILESSON

You may want to begin your minilesson reminding students of the work that they did in the previous day's session. Say something like, "Yesterday, you learned that writers edit to bring out specificity and intent (feelings, imagery, etc.). They consider craft moves that mentor authors make as they do this." You could ask them to locate a place in their writing where they made an edit the same way Jane Yolen edits, by replacing dull language with beautiful, precise language, language that helps the reader get a clear sense of what is going on. They can share this editing work with a partner.

Then you can continue your editing conversation, letting students in on other things that editors think about when they are getting ready for publication. You might say, "Today I want to teach you that writers who are preparing their pieces for an audience think about all of the things they have learned about editing, making sure they've gotten all of those things right, before sharing their work."

Then, in the teaching portion of the minilesson, you might hand out editing checklists to children that include all of the editing techniques they have been learning so far this year. You might include new things on the list today as well (perhaps you'll teach children that holidays and brand names are capitalized), or not. Either way, you'll remind children that this, too, is a resource for them as writers. Just as they've consulted Jane Yolen this month, now they will consult this editing checklist, being sure their writing is as clear and clean as it can be. You might then demonstrate how to fix up a piece of writing that you know has errors. This could be a portion of a child's piece of writing, or it could be one of your own, or it could be the class story. If you use one of the latter two cases, however, be sure in advance of today that you have made errors that mimic ones your second-graders tend to make. Then, demonstrate how you look between the editing checklist and the piece of writing to see what is and isn't working.

Then, you will turn the task over to students. You might have them work alone or in partnerships to try this out in their own writing. They should look at the pieces they selected yesterday and perhaps work on each partner's first page. They will be on the lookout for run-on sentences, for bits of text that don't make use of commas in a series of single words (e.g., lists), for missing end punctuation, for first words or names that aren't capitalized, for words whose spelling looks wrong, and for simple (high-frequency) words they have accidentally misspelled. Children can consult not only their editing checklists but any resource in the room that might help, such as the word wall or other books, charts, and texts they can find. For a word such as *laughing* they might consult a book in your room where they know that word is located. For a word such as *because* they can use the word wall.

As you send children off to edit the rest of the writing they have selected to share later today, you might voice over little reminders of the kinds of things they are looking for. Children can continue to consult their partners if need be, but this should be a quiet time, with each child concentrating on his or her work, editing as best he or she can.

CONFERRING AND SMALL-GROUP WORK

As children work, you will want to check in with them to be sure they are catching everything they can. Some children may say, after just five minutes, "I'm done!" Ask those children to show you what they found and fixed. Chances are they will have caught just a few things and there are more errors on their page. Point out something specific a child missed and then say something like, "I see something else you missed. Oops! There's another thing. See if you can find what I found. Use your editing checklist if you're not sure what to look for." Other children may have edited just one of the two pieces they intend to share, and will need reminders to edit their second piece. Of course, any student who feels like he or she has done all that can be done, independently, without feedback, can move on to editing and revising other pieces as well.

MID-WORKSHOP TEACHING

During the mid-workshop teaching, you might suggest that children come up with titles for their narratives. Teach them that the title should give the reader a hint of what the book will be about, that authors often come up with titles that mimic lines in the text or that paint a picture of some important part of the book. *Owl Moon*, for example, paints a picture of the night that Helen and her dad go out, and of the owl that they hope to see. By putting both words into her title, Jane conveys an image of both the setting and the focus of the adventure. Children could talk through some possible titles with a partner, pointing to sections of their text that support the ideas that they have. They could think about beautiful and precise language that factors into their pieces and might now be echoed in their titles.

SHARE

Finally, in the share, you and your students will celebrate! You could, of course, invite another second-grade class to be an audience, or you could set children up in their "writing circles" to share. Children can take turns talking about the craft moves they've tried out in their writing. Have they used any "Jane Yolens" particularly well, or have they tried out new craft moves? There won't be time for each child to read both pieces of writing (or even just one, since second-graders will tend to write long!), but students can pick out favorite sections or lines that reflect the craft moves they've tried out that make them particularly proud. The other members of the writing circle can interview the writer who is sharing, asking questions about intent and process. They might, for example, ask, "What made you choose that particular craft move?" or "What were you hoping the reader would get from this part of your story?"

Once they've shared what they've accomplished, you'll ask children to spend the rest of the share talking in their circles about their goals they set from the Narrative Writing Checklist. They can think back to the goals they set earlier during the unit, considering whether they have reached these. Then they can think forward, imagining new goals they hope to reach during the second portion of this unit. Do they hope to write with more detail in future pieces of writing? To write a more focused piece or to bring out the feelings more and use "show, not tell"? You will also want students reflecting and setting goals about how to use craft moves in the next part of the unit. Just like earlier, you will want children to write down these goals so that they can reflect once more on them toward the very end of the unit. This type of formative assessment not only allows students to set goals; it also guides you to plan instructional lessons to support the major needs in your classroom.

As you bring the celebration to a close, you might end with another Jane Yolen quotation. "Writers, Jane Yolen has said, 'All the books that I have ever read inspire my own writing'" (janeyolen.com). Have students turn and talk about what this quote means for them as writers. What books are they reading now? Are those books giving them ideas for things to try in their own writing? If you decide to end the celebration this way, you will create a nice bridge to the next session, in which students choose their own mentor texts.

Good luck,

Amanda and Julia

Learning Craft Moves
from Any Mentor Text

IN THIS SESSION, you'll teach students that writers can learn from any mentor author, at any time.

GETTING READY

✔ "How to Learn Writing Moves from a Mentor Text" chart (see Teaching)

✔ Teacher's demonstration piece of writing (see Teaching)

✔ *The Leaving Morning* by Angela Johnson, or another new mentor text to study with the class (see Teaching)

✔ Post-it notes (see Teaching)

✔ A basket of mentor texts for students to choose from (see Teaching and Mid-Workshop Teaching)

✔ Student Writing Folders (see Active Engagement)

✔ Students bring one piece of writing (see Share)

YOU AND YOUR CHILDREN HAVE ARRIVED at the final bend of this unit. In every unit of study we create, we build in scaffolds to support children as they learn new work—we guide them through the use of new strategies and processes. Often, we guide them for a few weeks to cycle repeatedly through the process of writing, from idea to finished piece and back again (and again). Then, after those few weeks of scaffolded practice, the time comes to remove some of the scaffolding. We withdraw some of the support because, of course, we need to teach children to use what they have learned even in contexts where they don't have a teacher's support. So, often in the final bend of a unit, you will see that we cycle students through the same processes again, set them up to use the same strategies again, this time with fewer scaffolds—with less support from the teacher.

At the end of this bend, then, you can expect that children will have enough experience using mentor texts that they can now turn to mentor texts on their own, in the world, when no teacher can be seen for miles around. After all, if we've not taught children something they can do without us, what have we really taught them? In this bend, then, you will lead children through the same moves they've worked through in Bends I and II, but you will now expect more independence. Where initially you chose the mentor text, in this bend, children will choose their own mentor texts. Where initially you helped children find a powerful part of that text, this time they'll find their own powerful part. Where initially you guided children through the use of the chart (to notice *what* is powerful, name *why* it is powerful, and figure out *how* to try a craft move), this time through you'll expect them to do that work on their own.

Today, you start teaching to increase independence by asking children to find their own mentor texts. Then, you ask them to study the selected texts on their own, in the same ways you studied a mentor text together in earlier sessions. Then, following the same process as earlier in the unit, you'll move on to a session where the children apply to their own writing the craft moves they've discovered in their mentor texts—on their own.

Learning Craft Moves from Any Mentor Text

CONNECTION

Use the example of learning to cross the street as a metaphor for learning to use mentor texts independently. Just as over time children need less and less support in crossing the street, so too, they will need less and less support learning from a mentor author.

"Writers, answer these questions in your mind, quietly. When you were a baby, how did you get from one side of the street to the other?" I paused for a second to let them answer in their minds. "I imagine you were pushed in a stroller, or were carried in someone's arms. Now think again—how did you get across the street when you were a bit older, when you were a kindergartner?" I paused. "I bet you went across the street holding someone's hand tightly, right? No one was carrying you anymore, you were walking on your own, but you still needed to hold a hand to get across safely. What about now? How does it go now?

"By now, you have learned mostly all the things you need to do to cross the street on your own, right? You know that you need to find a crosswalk, and look both ways until you see no cars, and if there is a light, wait for the signal that means walk. You know the whole process for how that goes, and I bet on some streets, you can walk across nearly all by yourself now, right? You've learned, little by little, the way to do that on your own.

"That's the way learning goes a lot of the time, isn't it? You get a lot of help for a while, and then you get a little less help and do more on your own. Then, finally, with a lot of practice and feedback, you do it yourself.

"It's like that in this unit, too. You've had a lot of practice learning how to use mentor texts as a writing resource. Now it is time to start doing this on your own, so that you do it all your life, even when no one is there to carry you or to hold your hand.

❖ **Name the teaching point.**

"Today I want to teach you that whenever you want some help with your writing, you can find it. Just choose a mentor text for yourself, and find what you admire, why you admire that part, and how the author wrote it. Then, try the same move in your writing."

The gradual release of responsibility model is not usually something we discuss with seven-year-olds, but if we're asking students to assume more responsibility and we can help them understand the game plan, why not?

TEACHING

Tell writers that whenever they want help improving their writing, they can call on the services of a mentor author. Review the chart listing steps for doing so.

"All your life, there will be times when you look at your writing and think, 'Hmmm. This could be better.' You'll want to call out, 'Help!' But oftentimes, no one will be nearby to help. Here's the good news. You can always think, 'Help is on the way.' Because as writers, you now know how to help yourselves. You've learned to do so in this unit. Let's review what you learned at the very start of the unit and make sure you are ready to do this work on your own.'" I revealed the "How to Learn Writing Moves from a Mentor Text" chart:

> ### How to Learn Writing Moves from a Mentor Text
>
> 1. Choose a text you admire, reread it.
> 2. Notice what is a powerful part.
> 3. Name why it is a powerful part.
> 4. Figure out how the author does it and then try it in your own writing.

"Does this look familiar? We made a chart of 'what, why, and how' to help us study *Owl Moon*. We did this work together as a class, but today I want you to know that you can do this all on your own, anytime you want."

Demonstrate how you call on the help of a mentor author so that children will self-initiate this work in ways that improve their writing.

"Let me show you how I call on the help of a mentor author, and then, during writing time, you'll all have a chance to do this as well." I sat back and straightened up, to show I was entering into the demonstration. "Hmm, here I am writing my story about the ocean, and I want help making it an even stronger story. So . . . (I tapped the first line on the chart) I'm going to find a teacher! Let me look through this basket of beautiful, well written books that we've read over and over again." I leafed through the basket. "Here it is! *The Leaving Morning*." I held it up. "I've read this book many times and Angela Johnson is a writer whose work I admire.

"Now, before this text can help me as a writer, I need to reread it (and I tapped the word *reread* on the chart). And while I reread it, I will keep in mind that I'm going to look for a powerful part." I pointed to the second step on our chart.

"I need to notice what is a powerful part, name why it is powerful, and figure out how Angela Johnson does it."

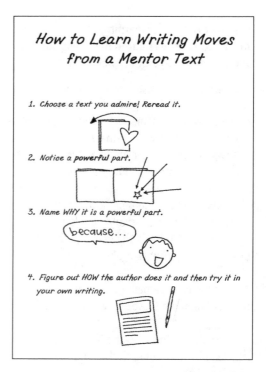

How to Learn Writing Moves from a Mentor Text

1. Choose a text you admire! Reread it.
2. Notice a *powerful* part.
3. Name WHY it is a powerful part.
   because...
4. Figure out HOW the author does it and then try it in your own writing.

I began to read the book aloud, and then stopped a few pages in. "Second-graders, you know what? One part that stands out to me as powerful is the beginning part, this part. I'll put it up on the document camera."

The LEAVING happened on a soupy, misty morning.

when you could hear the street sweeper.

Sssshhhshsh . . .

"I've noticed what is a powerful part, but now I have to ask myself, '*Why* is that part so powerful?' Hmmm . . . I think Angela does something Jane does as well. She writes in a way that makes me feel like I'm right there, like I'm part of the story. A 'soupy, misty morning . . .' I can feel just how hot and steamy it is, like one of those sticky summer mornings in the city. Also, she has set a mood—a feeling—quiet and sort of sad." I tapped the "why" portion of a blank chart.

ACTIVE ENGAGEMENT

Recruit children's help thinking about how the author made a part powerful, and name the craft moves she used that they can try, too.

"And finally, I need to think about how Angela made that part so powerful. Hmmm . . .

"Think with me, 'How does Angela do it?' Talk with your partner for a moment—name some ways she made this beginning powerful, memorable, interesting." I paused for a moment and listened in as children named craft moves they saw in the excerpt.

"Okay, I know you aren't finished, but I heard so many of you naming what Angela does, and you also noticed that some of it is like what Jane Yolen does, right?"

I ticked off their observations on my fingers as I said them aloud.

"Angela uses unusual words like *soupy* to show the mood. Isn't that interesting—'a *soupy* morning'?! Hey, look—Angela uses another unusual phrase: *The Leaving Morning*. I've never heard someone refer to a morning that way."

"She also uses sounds! She says, 'ssssshhhhh.' It's like the 'whooo-whooo' in *Owl Moon*."

"You are right that these are craft moves I could try if I want to set the mood in my own writing. I'll use a Post-it to mark that place in *The Leaving Morning* so that I can remember to do those things. On my Post-it I'll jot down *mood* since that is why I would do it and then I'll write *unusual words* and *sounds* so that I know how to do it. Thanks for your help!"

Notice here that I name a new craft move—setting a mood—as if it is something the class has already studied. Because, by now, we have done so much work around setting, adding details to pull the reader in, and writing to evoke a particular feeling, I know that children will understand what I mean by mood.

This is complicated work—noticing what an author has done and why. You are immersing them in work that they can grow into over the years.

LINK

Give students an opportunity to reread their writing and plan with their partners. Then remind them that they can use the chart to help them learn from a mentor text of their choice.

"So writers, be as independent as you can be today, as you work on your writing. Pull out a piece of writing from the unfinished side of your folder right now." I gave them a few seconds to do this. "Look for a place where you may have hit some trouble, where you may want to make your writing more powerful. Thumbs-up if you are ready to work on that part of your writing, like you just helped me work on my ocean story." Thumbs popped up.

"If you are ready to take in a lesson from a mentor author, try it on your own, using the chart to help you remember the steps. Off you go!"

Going Back to Basics with Your Conferences and Small Groups

A S YOU CONFER, YOU MAY FIND that some students feel stymied by parts of the process they learned earlier in the unit. Sometimes you will find a student who only wants to write one story, over and over again. Stephen was such a student. He only wanted to write about Beyblades. Stephen had actually written a wonderful narrative about playing with his father, but now he said he couldn't think of any other stories. I reminded Stephen of other strategies, besides thinking of things he had done, to help him generate a story idea. I reminded him that he could also think about places he had been. This strategy often jogs the memory and conjures up new types of story. It did just that for Stephen. He thought of countless stories he could tell about Ireland and decided to tell one about when he got caught in a rainstorm in a bog near his grandparents' farmhouse (see Figure 15–1). In fact, this strategy worked so well that Stephen remembered the details that made that moment stand out—ones that he included in his new story. Even though it is late in the unit, don't be afraid to bring back old strategies.

(continues)

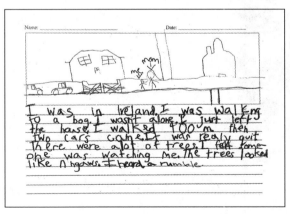

I was in Ireland. I was walking to a bog. I wasn't alone. I just left the house. I walked 400m then two cars came. It was really quiet. There were a lot of trees. I felt someone was watching me. The trees looked like ninjas. I heard a rumble.

FIG. 15–1 Stephen's writing

MID-WORKSHOP TEACHING
Choosing Your Own Mentor Text

I interrupted as students were working. "One two three, eyes on me!"

"One two eyes on you," they called in response.

"Writers, I need to share something very important with you. I am noticing that some of you are coming over to the basket of possible mentor texts, thumbing through it, and then walking away with nothing. Why is that?"

"I'm not really sure how to pick which book to use," Chloe responded.

"Are others feeling the same way?" I asked. Many heads nodded in agreement. "Okay then, let me tell you about how *I* pick a mentor text. The first thing I do is look through books I know really well. I can't make a book a mentor text if I haven't read it before. When I made this basket, I filled it with beautiful books that we have shared together for read-alouds, so most of you should know most of the books in the basket. But if you were absent on the day we read one, or out of the classroom for something, then there may be a book in there you don't know. That is probably not a good choice for you. Another thing I think about is how I *feel* about the book. I have to love a book to want to study it, pull it apart, make careful jottings about it. And finally, I think about whether I could write like this author. Is Angela Johnson the type of writer I could write like? Or maybe Mem Fox is more my style. So these are the things to think about when choosing a mentor text. For the rest of the writing time, I'll hover near the basket of books. If you want a little more guidance in choosing a mentor text, I'll be around to help."

There are a few important things to remember that will help you run small groups in your writing workshop. The first is, make sure you actually do them. Some teachers say, "I just don't have time to know which children to gather together, or what to say." Others say, "I don't have time to plan small groups." The truth is there is always a reason for not doing almost anything—but small-group work is non-negotiable. So the real solution is to figure out what you need in order to find a way to lead these groups regularly.

If you are unsure of which students to gather together or what to teach, know that studying—and categorizing—student work often will help with this decision. Notice patterns across students' work, and record the needs you see. Then, in the workshop, carry notes from this study time alongside you. You may ask, "What do I look for in student work?" First, notice whatever has been a priority in your teaching. In this unit, notice the craft moves that students use and whether they use these consistently. Also, notice what a student seems to be trying to do, even if he or she doesn't yet have a full

understanding or control of that thing. Lastly, look to see what the student is *not* using that would help improve his or her writing. As you study your student data, teaching points will begin to emerge.

As you pull your small groups, make sure that your students know what they are doing well and encourage them to continue doing whatever is working. You may decide to teach into whatever it is that they are gesturing towards or that they already use but use inconsistently. This is a great place to start teaching, because it indicates a student's "zone of proximal development."

When you have questions around small-group work, don't be afraid to reach out to your colleagues to find out how they handle similar matters. But don't let your questions or busy schedule keep you from leading these. It is essential that you use this format of teaching to help kids who could use this more focused attention.

Sharing Favorite Parts of Writing

Ask children to choose a part of their writing that they would love to share.

"Do you remember how, at the start of the year, you all brought small treasures to school—acorns and pretty stones—and showed them during 'Show and Tell'? Today we're going to have another show and tell. We're going to bring out our small treasures and show them to each other. But they'll be small treasures we find in our *writing*, not physical objects from home. Before we start our sharing, could you reread your writing and find a detail you love, a detail that is a small treasure, and would you star it?"

The room was silent while children reread. As they started to look back up, I said, "Now think about what makes the part you selected treasure. See if you can find words to describe why that part feels so special to you."

I gave students another minute to think before calling on a few to share with the class. As they shared, I modeled intent, responsive listening, and made sure that kids in the class were following my lead. I said things like, "Eyes on . . ." or, to the child sharing, "Wait till you can hear a pin drop. Read it like this is gold."

After kids had shared, I said, "Writers, listen to all that treasure! I bet it's given you ideas for what you might do next in your writing. Right now, turn to your partner and describe one small bit of treasure that's waiting for you to explore next.

"Okay, off you go to hunt for treasure!"

There was like 48 people for the bus. And we had a little car that came up to the window. And it was a little race car and we were so close. "Wow, this is taking forever," and I was mad.

The water was cool but I had to go with my dad. My dad spinned me around on the sea there was thrilling of people. I was shocked at the medium wave. I glared at it! The wave pushed me. I try to hesitate but I couldn't. So I got to my dad he help me swim. Cause I couldn't swim. I had such a spectacular time! Great stuff happens a lot.

Title: My First Day of School
The first time when I came into the school year I was shivering. I was biting my lip. When I got on the line I was standing still.

Fig. 15–2 These three pieces show a strength in how each writer is working on using details to show what was happening and how they were feeling.

Being Bold
Trying New Craft Moves

IN THIS SESSION, you'll teach children that writers are bold. They try new things in their writing, even if they aren't perfect at these, and then they decide if the new things they tried work.

GETTING READY

✔ Student writing from previous session, marked with Post-it notes to signify places where they are trying out craft moves, and a pen (see Connection)

✔ Your own writing (see Teaching)

✔ *The Leaving Morning* by Angela Johnson, or another mentor text (see Teaching)

✔ "Learning Writing Moves from Our Favorite Authors" chart and Narrative Writing Checklist, Grades 2 and 3 (see Link)

✔ A student piece of writing and mentor text (see Share)

T HROUGHOUT THIS UNIT, you have shown your students how to learn through example. Children have had repeated opportunities to conduct a close study of a carefully selected powerful text, and they've repeatedly noticed how an author writes, speculating on how the authorial devices support the text's meaning.

Continuing the previous session's push for independence, you'll suggest that children try out the craft moves that they identified in their mentor texts. Whereas earlier in the unit, children worked largely in concert, with every child trying the same craft moves in unison, today—and for the rest of the unit—they will be working essentially on their own, each child finding inspiration in his or her own mentor.

Today is all about being bold. We cannot emphasize enough how important it is that children experiment. The last thing you want is a class of dutiful writers who robotically proceed to implement a handful of craft moves and then call a piece "done."

Stress to your class that writers don't just try out one craft move and then magically poof! A perfect draft is born. Rather, writers try out a variety of things, in a number of ways and places in their writing, looking for the right fit. Perhaps children will begin by emulating an "Angela Johnson" or a "Kevin Henkes" or a "Cynthia Rylant."

As the unit nears a close, you'll want children to begin to take ownership of their own craft decisions and writing moves. After all, in just a few days, they will be crowned a new class of master writers!

Being Bold
Trying New Craft Moves

CONNECTION

Ask students to revisit the writing they did in the prior session, reflecting on the craft moves they learned from their new mentor authors.

"Writers, on your way over to the meeting area today, please bring the story from your folder that you're working on right now, the Post-it notes you've written about craft moves your mentor authors have made, and a pen. If you haven't yet incorporated any new craft moves into your writing, bring the writing that you are currently working on. When you get to your rug spot, begin to reread your story carefully. Remind yourself what you are trying to show the reader or get the reader to think in each part."

You begin the minilesson by asking students to engage in the work you've been teaching them—a wonderful way to remind them of prior teaching without droning on about what you've taught.

As students did this, I walked around the meeting area, coaching them to think about what kinds of images, feelings, and/or thoughts they were trying to show in their writing.

After a few minutes, I began to voice over students' intentions, to help those who were still thinking about their own: "Rocio is trying to write a really scary story, Eric is writing an 'LOL' story that he hopes will make his reader laugh a lot, and Isabelle found a really serious topic that she hopes will make her reader think—her story is about lying!"

By naming what some children are doing, you give others models.

Set the stage for children to take risks as they write.

"Yesterday, you each spent a lot of time studying your own mentor author. You all noticed and named many things you saw your author doing to make his or her writing powerful. Some of you found things your writer does that are a lot like what Jane and Angela do as writers. Some of you found things that your author does that *neither* Jane nor Angela do!

"But when I asked you how you were going to try to do the things you noticed in your own writing, many of you said, 'I don't know how.'" I shrugged my shoulders and let my hands collapse onto my lap with a big emphasis. "It's like you gave up! Someone even said to me, 'What if I do it wrong?' And then I thought to myself, 'Aha! Now I understand. It can be a little scary to write in new ways.'

"Can I tell you a secret?" I leaned forward and gestured for them to lean in closer. In a whisper voice I said, "It happens all the time to grown-up writers! All writers get scared! But the great thing about writing is that you can try something on and if it doesn't fit, you can just take it off and try something new. Like trying a new coat. Sometimes it doesn't fit right, or you don't like the color or style. So you take it off and try a new one on to see if that one's a better match. Writing is the same."

❖ Name the teaching point.

"Today I want to teach you that when writers do something new, they don't just try it once and give up. Writers are bold! You can be bold too. You can try new things in your writing, even if they're not perfect. Then you can see what you think. You can ask yourself, 'Did it work?' or 'Should I try it again in a new way?'"

TEACHING

Demonstrate trying something new you learned from a mentor author. Model first how daunting this can be.

"Let's take another look at my ocean story, and I'll show you how I go about trying out one thing and then another to see what works best. Remember how I wanted to show how terrified I was, especially when I was underneath the water? Let me just reread that part of the story here, to remind you how it goes."

> I called out to Frances, but it was too loud for her to hear. I did a little half dive. Then the wave tumbled me down, down, down.

"I like this part of my story, but I'm not sure it gets across to my reader how terrified I was. I was so scared! Hmm, . . . I know! I can look at my mentor text, *The Leaving Morning*, and see if I spot any craft moves that might help me make my story more powerful—to draw out how terrified I was." I leafed through the book, looking at the places I had marked with Post-it notes. "Hmm, . . . I could repeat a phrase like Angela did. She kept writing 'leaving morning' and 'left lips.' That's one of the things I marked the other day. But how would I use that in my piece?" I said this with a heavy sigh, and a defeated look on my face. "We haven't practiced it yet."

"Try it! Try it!" Some kids egged me on.

Model how to be bold, trying out a craft move in several different ways until the writing feels just right.

"Okay, I will try! I will be bold." I took a deep breath. "I could repeat 'big wave.' Hmm, . . . No, that doesn't feel as poetic as 'leaving morning' and 'left lips' and it doesn't really let my reader know how scared I was." I pretended to take off a coat. "That is not a good match for me."

"'Drowning!' You could write 'the drowning water,'" Alex called out.

"Hmm," I said. "I could try that. I gestured as if trying on a new coat. "'The drowning water.' That has an interesting ring! Sounds a lot like 'the leaving morning,' doesn't it? It's definitely dramatic and scary! Or"—I gestured one more time trying on a new coat—"I could have the wave roar again and again. Or repeat 'the deep, dark water.' I got in alliteration in that last one! All of those would work to show how terrified I was.

"Writers, do you see how I tried out different ways to use this new craft move to show how scared I was in my story? I didn't give up. I was bold and tried on a few different things. It may not be perfect—yet. But that's okay. This is going to help me not only try new things; eventually it will help me find exactly what I want my writing to say."

ACTIVE ENGAGEMENT

Ask students to find a craft move from their own mentor texts, and then help you incorporate it into your story.

"Your turn, writers. Open up your mentor texts. Find some of the things that your mentor did. How can your author help me with my ocean story? Let's be bold and just try it out, even if it is not perfect!"

"Partner 1, share with Partner 2. What could we try in this part of the ocean story to show how terrified I was? If you are still not sure, Partner 2 can help you think about some examples."

Debrief, highlighting some of the work that partners did to revise your story.

"Writers, you are coming up with a lot of options! Gabriela, for example, realized that I could do what Kevin Henkes does in *Kitten's First Full Moon* (2004). He does something that Jane does too, she realized. He stretches out his story and makes the reader wait, wait, wait and hope, hope, hope, too. But he does it by using ellipses—dot dot dot. He shows you all the places where the kitten goes. Gabriela suggested that in my ocean story I could write, 'The wave came closer and closer. It passed over my friend Frances . . . it moved past the clouds in the sky . . . it came right over my head.' She could probably do the same thing in her ballet piece that she brought to the meeting area!"

LINK

Send students off to try out what they've learned from their mentor authors in their own writing.

"As you write today, you will need your books, folders, paper, Post-it notes, and pens. Feel free to use *all* the tools in our writing center and here in the meeting area." I pointed to the "Learning Writing Moves from Our Favorite Authors" chart, the *Leaving Morning* Post-it notes, and the Narrative Writing Checklist.

Notice that you need not actually decide upon or record your revision. The point is to demonstrate the process of trying alternatives.

Here is another example of how to teach students to reflect on their writing and set goals. Although I do not ask them to specifically set goals and write these down, they are still doing the work of rereading their writing through the lens of self-assessment, noticing the choices they have made as writers and pushing themselves to write in different ways to improve their pieces.

Learning Writing Moves from Our Favorite Authors

WHAT is powerful?	WHY is it powerful?	HOW is it done?
Page 1 of <u>Owl Moon</u>	feels like you are there	names what character exactly: • sees • hears • feels

Right before owl
 arrives in <u>Owl Moon</u>,
 when the father
 calls out to it
	you wonder what will
	 happen next, and hope
	 things turn out a certain
	 way
		makes a comparison
		 • uses actions and
		   images that show a
		   character hopes for
		   something
		 • gives clues that
		   something might
		   happen
		 • stretches out the
		   story. The big thing
		   doesn't happen
		   right away.

showing the big idea in <u>Owl Moon</u> (pp. 11, 13, 29)	lets the reader know what is most important	uses repetition

"Why don't you start thinking about trying your same craft move in your own piece? Start now, here in the meeting area. When you've tried it once or twice, head to your writing spots and continue working! You have many writing teachers today. Don't forget to study these and then write with power and precision!"

Focusing on the Most Important Strategies Students Should Be Taking Away

As YOU CONFER, it will be important for you to keep your eye on what matters most and to be willing to let go of what doesn't. For example, it matters that children look at the work of another author and come to their own observations about what that author has done and why. You can't expect children will come up with observations or insights as astute as those that you'd make! Be willing to let children do their seven- and eight-year-old best. Just as children need to approximate when they spell, they also need to approximate when they study the craftsmanship in a book. Then, too, it matters that your children look at their own writing and think not only about *what* they will say but also about *how* they will write. It matters that they deliberately use craft moves they've admired in the work of other authors, that they try to use interesting techniques as they write, and that they reread their own writing, listening for the sounds of their language. If they do all this and yet add only sound words (and overuse even those!), don't be discouraged.

Even when children are only approximating, you can see what they've done that is smart and name it for them. Try, also, to think of just one step forward a child might make, and to teach just that. The pattern in your conferences will be to research, to give a compliment, to make a suggestion, and then to send the child off with a reminder of how he or she can use that suggestion not just today, in this piece, but also tomorrow, and in future pieces.

MID-WORKSHOP TEACHING
Transferring Craft Moves across One's Writing

"Writers, one two three, eyes on me!" Students called back, "One two, eyes on you!" Once I had their attention, I said, "You've been working so hard on your writing. I can tell that you've been bold, trying out new craft moves from our mentor texts. I saw Patrick repeating a phrase in a couple of places in his text, and I saw Grace adding descriptive details and sound words in her story. I want to tell you something very important. You might feel tired. You might think, 'Well, I tried that move once, I'm done now.' But writers don't just try a craft move once and then forget about it. No way! They try that craft move in many places in their story, and even in other stories they are writing.

"Right now, will you choose one of the craft moves you have been working on today? Then, look through your story to see where else you might do the same thing. You might even go back to stories you wrote earlier in the unit and begin to revise those, since what you know as a writer now is so much more than what you knew at the beginning of the year! Okay, writers, back to work!"

Learning from Mentor Authors

Ask a child to share the work he has done under the mentorship of a new author. Ask the student questions to probe for more information.

"Writers, I am so proud of the work you did today on your stories. I want to share something that one of you has done that I think is really special, and that could help you as you continue drafting your pieces.

"Brandon, will you share with us what you did in your writing?"

Brandon said, "My story is about going to Central Park. I love it there. It is my favorite park. I tried to make my story like Cynthia Rylant."

"How did you do that?" I asked.

"I wrote about all the things that we did. Then when it was over, I said, 'I was dreaming about it in my home.' Just like Cynthia Rylant did."

"Is that what she does?"

Brandon responded by reading Rylant's ending to *The Relatives Came*.

> *And when They were finally home in Virginia, they crawled into their silent, soft beds and dreamed about the next summer.*

Ask the class to notice ways in which the child's writing was similar to the published writing.

"Now read us your piece. Let's listen to Brandon's story (see Figure 16–1) and see what we notice. Then, Brandon, you can tell us where you got that idea from. Maybe it came from Cynthia Rylant? Or another author? Or maybe it was just *your* idea." Brandon read it aloud.

> Once I went to Central Park. It was sunny but it was cold. We played football and soccer. Central Park is my . . . I pretend it is a house and a shop and a gas station. Central Park is my favorite park.

I am very thoughtful about how I choose a student to spotlight. Usually, I choose a student with whom I conferred that day, ensuring the work he did teaches the rest of the class something. Sometimes I choose a student who has tried a strategy that can be helpful for other writers. Other times I choose a student who had difficulties we worked together to problem solve in a way I hope other students will emulate. I also try not to call on the same students over and over, so that the rest of the class doesn't feel as if they are not spotlight-worthy.

I have a tree house in Central Park. It is so cool . . .

We had a big race! I won! But my cousins got in front of me. Central Park is my favorite park.

Then we went back home. We watched TV! for 2 hours then we went to sleep. I dreamed about going to Central Park.

Ask the class to notice ways in which the child's writing was similar to the published writing.

Anna said, "I like your repeating line. Central Park is important to your story. Who gave you that idea?"

"I got that from *The Relatives Came* too," Brandon replied.

"Everyone, tell your partner what else you notice." After partners shared, we named a couple more things we noticed in Brandon's piece. For each one, I opened up *The Relatives Came* to show how it mirrored one of Rylant's craft moves.

"Writers, now turn to your partner and share what *you* did today in your writing. Show each other both your piece of writing and also the books you studied. Find what is the same."

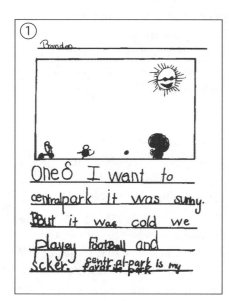

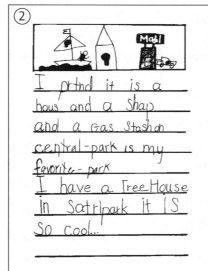

One day I went to Central Park. It was sunny, but it was cold. We played football and soccer. Central Park is my favorite park.

I pretend it is a house and a shop and a gas station. Central Park is my favorite park. I have a tree house in Central Park. It is so cool…

We had a big race! I won! But my cousins were in front of me. Central Park is my favorite park.

Then we went back home. We watched TV! for 2 hours then we went to sleep. I dreamed about going to Central Park.

FIG. 16–1   Brandon's writing shows how he studied and used his own mentor author.

Writers Can Help Each Other

Partners Offer Feedback

ear Teachers,

Just as you've taught children to turn to their own mentor books and authors for suggestions during this bend, in this session you'll remind them that they have another resource for inspiration: their writing partners. Many professional writers have a community of writer friends to whom they turn for feedback, both when they are developing an idea, and later, when they are revising. They bounce ideas and writing off one another, posing questions, reflecting on what is—and isn't yet—working, and checking to be sure that their writing has the effect they intended. Likewise, you'll suggest that partners can play the same role for each other. Of course, children have been working with partners from Day One, so this won't be new work exactly. To give it a fresh angle, you'll announce that partners can be a writer's best resource, offering fresh eyes and fresh insight.

MINILESSON

In your connection, you might say, "Writers, from the very beginning of this unit, you've learned how to consult professional writers. You've looked to them for craft ideas, for revision techniques, and for inspiration. You've mentored yourselves to Jane Yolen and Angela Johnson, to Kevin Henkes, Cynthia Rylant, and Donald Crews. Today, you're going to apprentice yourselves to other master writers. You're going to apprentice yourselves to—each other!"

Keep your teaching point lean and concise, and word it in a way that indicates this is something your students can draw on again and again, not just today. You might say something like, "Today I want to teach you that even the masters turn to other writers for help. They ask each other questions and check that their writing is as clear, meaningful, and well crafted as it can be. Writers revise in the company of other writers. And you and your writing partner can do the same."

For your demonstration, you might elicit the help of one child in the class, setting her up to act as your writing partner. Arrange with the child in advance of the workshop so that she is prepared for the sort of exchange you'll demonstrate for the rest of the class, and so that she comes to the rug with writing goals and a piece of writing.

During the demo, invite the child to have a seat next to you, at the front of the rug, and put the Narrative Writing Checklist on the overhead, for the whole class to see. Announce that both you and your "writing partner" will quickly look between the goals she set earlier this unit and the piece of writing she is currently revising, checking to see that she's done what she set out to do. Take just thirty seconds to do this. Then ask the child to reflect on the ways in which she has met her writing goals. Perhaps she set out to bring her writing to life by telling what the people in it are thinking and feeling, and by using descriptive words. She can decide if she's done that in ways that do, in fact, breathe life into her writing.

Next, you might ask her to consider new goals, using the Narrative Writing Checklist. Perhaps she'll decide to aim for similar things but in more parts of her writing, or to focus next on crafting an ending or beginning in a new way. Try to steer the writer to reach for goals that feel both doable and

Narrative Writing Checklist

	Grade 2	NOT YET	STARTING TO	YES!	Grade 3	NOT YET	STARTING TO	YES!
	Structure				**Structure**			
Overall	I wrote about *one time* when I did something.	☐	☐	☐	I told the story bit by bit.	☐	☐	☐
Lead	I thought about how to write a good beginning and chose a way to start my story. I chose the action, talk, or setting that would make a good beginning.	☐	☐	☐	I wrote a beginning in which I helped readers know who the characters were and what the setting was in my story.	☐	☐	☐
Transitions	I told the story in order by using words such as *when, then,* and *after*.	☐	☐	☐	I told my story in order by using phrases such as *a little later* and *after that*.	☐	☐	☐
Ending	I chose the action, talk, or feeling that would make a good ending.	☐	☐	☐	I chose the action, talk, or feeling that would make a good ending and worked to write it well.	☐	☐	☐
Organization	I wrote a lot of lines on a page and wrote across a lot of pages.	☐	☐	☐	I used paragraphs and skipped lines to separate what happened first from what happened later (and finally) in my story.	☐	☐	☐
	Development				**Development**			
Elaboration	I tried to bring my characters to life with details, talk, and actions.	☐	☐	☐	I worked to show what happened to (and in) my characters.	☐	☐	☐
Craft	I chose strong words that would help readers picture my story.	☐	☐	☐	I not only told my story, but also wrote it in ways that got readers to picture what was happening and that brought my story to life.	☐	☐	☐

cognitively higher level, so that the rest of the class sees that writers aim to tackle harder work as they become more skilled. Of course, this is just one suggestion for demonstrating how writers rely on other writers to discuss and set goals for their writing, and make revision plans. You may think of other ways that work better for your students.

For the active engagement, children could meet in partnerships to carry on similar conversations. As they talk, call out little coaching tips, or circulate the room, whispering in suggestions. Children who tend to focus solely on one kind of goal may need reminders to think about other categories. Children who set out to do everything on the checklist may benefit from focusing on fewer goals, trying these out in more places in their writing, or in more substantial ways. Coach into the ways in which partnerships talk, too, making sure that these are as productive as they can be. Remind children to be active listeners and talkers, to take turns in each role, to build on each other's ideas rather than just offering their own thoughts, and to take into consideration each other's intentions as writers as they talk.

As you send children off to write, suggest that they now have lots of thinking to carry with them. Remind them that not only can they consider goals they might have set from the Narrative Writing Checklist, they can also revisit other tools and charts the class has created over the course of this unit, such as the craft chart. Finally, tell them that if they need to touch base with their partner again, they can take a turn in the partnership corner (and be sure to set up two chairs for this purpose).

CONFERRING AND SMALL-GROUP WORK

As you confer with children today, give special attention to the ways in which you are giving feedback; are you being as precise and honest as you can be about what is and isn't working? Are your compliments specific and poignant? Are they worded in such a way that kids can replicate the work? Consider, too, how you talk to children about their goals. You may want to push them to create ones that are bigger than the ones they name and that transfer across units. That is, although some goals will certainly be narrative-specific, others might be about editing or about organization or stretching out an important part or about volume, and could just as easily apply to work in an information unit of study as they do to this one.

MID-WORKSHOP TEACHING

For your mid-workshop teaching, you might suggest that partners could quickly check in with each other, showing how they've taken each other's advice or begun to work on a goal.

SHARE

Then, for the share, you might suggest that partners not only give advice, but also listen as readers. Children might again meet with their partners, this time reading each other's writing as readers and then reacting to it. Patrick decided that one of his goals was to write with more details. He thought that he needed to work on giving more information as he wrote. In this example (see Figure 17–1), Patrick zoomed in on entering the birdhouse. His partner, Brandon, was elated by his details. You could hear him call out from the other side of the meeting area, "Whoa! No way!" Patrick knew his details were working. Children can see whether the way in which their partner reacts is what they intended. Then they can use this information and advice and make new decisions about revisions to make for the next day.

Good luck,
Amanda and Julia

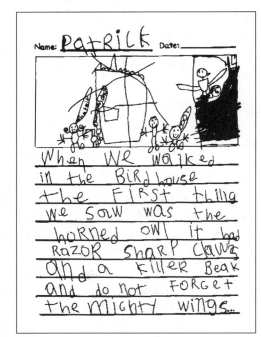

When we walked in the Bird house the first thing we saw was the horned owl. It had razor sharp claws and a killer beak and do not forget the mighty wings.

I felt like I wanted to dive into the cage. But couldn't. It is illegal.

FIG. 17–1   Patrick's writing shows how he has worked on his goal: writing more information and details.

Session 18

Editing and Preparing for Publication

ODAY IS THE SECOND TO LAST DAY of the unit, and you and your children have important work to do! In the last session students revised a couple of stories by reflecting on their goals, working with partnerships, and using all the charts and tools in the classroom. Now is their last opportunity to edit for punctuation, spelling, commas, capitals, and word choice. The work today is also an opportunity to help children develop a larger repertoire of editing strategies.

The beginning of the year is a wonderful opportunity to draw a strong link with your word study/phonics program to support your young writers in developing a repertoire of spelling strategies that help them not only fix up their spelling, but also transfer the skills that they are learning during another part of the day. You will want to analyze your students' writing so that you ensure the instruction you provide during word study and writing workshop supports students in reaching end-of-year expectations. Specifically, check that this instruction supports their knowledge of spelling-sound correspondences for common vowel teams, their use of these learned spelling patterns when they write words, and the continuation of the work they learned in first grade of spelling frequently occurring words correctly. Your students are at a transitional stage for spelling, a time when they will become more fluent as they learn many patterns designed to help them problem solve words more efficiently. You'll want to assess and plan instruction that develops your students' knowledge of word features, sight words, and word-solving strategies. You will do all of this with the goal of helping students become efficient problem solvers of words as they write, just as they are doing as they read.

You will likely emphasize the strategy of problem solving syllable by syllable in the first few months of school because each syllable has a vowel and so much of your work this year will support students in writing these vowel sounds, eventually with accuracy. You can demonstrate how you listen for and record a letter or letters for each vowel and then reread to check that each syllable will be read with the correct vowel sound (again, any vowel marker may be used when students are at the beginning stages of this work). This is a great opportunity to work with students on distinguishing between short and long vowel sounds.

IN THIS SESSION, you'll teach children that writers get their writing ready for publication by making sure it is easy to read. This means that they check their spelling, punctuation, and word choice.

GETTING READY

✔ White boards and markers, one for each student, to be brought to the meeting area

✔ "How Did I Make My Writing Easy to Read?" editing checklist

Editing and Preparing for Publication

CONNECTION

Remind children of all they have learned about editing, both this year and last.

"Writers and editors, on your way over to the meeting area, you will need a marker and a white board. When you have your materials, meet me on the rug.

"We have just one more day to get ready for our celebration tomorrow and there is still a lot of work ahead." I took out the "How Did I Make My Writing Easy to Read?" editing checklist. "You have been working on editing your pieces throughout this unit. Not only have you learned editing strategies from first grade, but you have also learned a few new things to look out for this year. With your partner, can you name what things are really important to do in editing, and how you do some of those things in your own writing? That is, can you give your partner some good tips about editing? Go ahead, turn and teach your partner about editing." As partners talked, I listened in.

"Wow! You really know a lot about editing. Brandon told his partner he uses books to help him think about his ending punctuation. Anna said that she rereads her work a couple of times. On the first read, she edits for capitalization and on the second read she edits for spelling. Tenzing said that she tries to fix punctuation in a sentence by trying it two or three different ways!

✦ Name the teaching point.

"As you fix up your writing for publication, it is important to be sure it is easy to read. Today I want to teach you that you can use strategies you are learning in word study to help you fix up your spelling. Specifically, you can think about the parts of words, listen to each syllable, and think, 'Is this part spelled with a short or long vowel sound?' Then you can try a few different spellings to see which sounds and looks best."

Turn-and-talks like this not only allow students to refresh their memories about the work they have learned, but also give you a chance to assess which students may need more support with this work. You can get a sense of which students you can pull together in a small group and which students may need some conferring support.

TEACHING

Model how to edit for spelling by breaking a word down into syllables and thinking about the vowel sounds in each one.

"Last night, I read through a few of your stories and pulled out some words for us to work on as a class to try out this strategy. Here is the first word: 'Babn.' This is the word *baboon*. Let's count how many syllables this word has; clap it out with me first." We clapped the two syllables.

"Two!" Grace shouted.

"Now, let's look at the first syllable, 'bab.' Do we need a short or long vowel? I think short, 'baaaaaab.' Now, let me hear the last part, 'ooooooon.' Long or short? Thumbs up for long, thumbs down for short." The children all gave a thumbs-up. "Yes, that is a long vowel. But, there are no vowels here! I need to write one in. What are the ways I know how to make the 'oooooo' sound? I could make it 'ue' like cue, 'oo' like balloon, or 'ew' like new."

"Double 'o'! I know it!" Isabelle called out.

"In this word it is a double 'o.' I'll add that.

"See how we thought about each syllable and about what kind of vowel—short or long—needed to be in each one? Let's try that with a few more words."

ACTIVE ENGAGEMENT

Set students up to work on the spelling of a second misspelled word, thinking about each syllable and the vowel sounds in each part.

"Ready for the next word?"

On the white board, I wrote, "ristrant."

"The word is *restaurant*. Let's clap out that word together. Rest-aur-ant. Caps off, white boards on your laps! Give it a try.

Editing Checklist

	How Did I Make My Writing Easy to Read?	NOT YET	STARTING TO	YES!
Spelling	To spell a word, I used what I knew about spelling patterns (*tion*, *er*, *ly*, and so on).	☐	☐	☐
	I spelled all of the word wall words correctly and used the word wall to help me figure out how to spell other words.	☐	☐	☐
Punctuation	I used quotation marks to show what characters said.	☐	☐	☐
	When I used words such as *can't* and *don't*, I put in the apostrophe.	☐	☐	☐

"Now, think about that first syllable. Long or short? Write it down. Listen to the next part. Is the vowel in the next part long or short? Write it down. Listen to the last part again. Is the vowel in the last syllable long or short? Write it down the best you can. When you are done, put your caps on and hold up your boards. Everyone, look around and see if we all agree."

I then wrote the word correctly underneath the misspelled word. As I did, I talked about how students could think about the spelling of the first syllable, "rest." There was a vowel in the misspelled word, but it was a short *i* sound, not a short *e* sound. The next part, "aur," sounds a bit like "er," which lots of kids had written.

"Lots of you put in a short *e* sound here—and I know why. It sounds a bit like that when you say it quickly, but listen closely again." I said the word slowly, emphasizing the second syllable. "Hear how that's more of an 'or' sound? In this case, it's spelled 'aur' like *dinosaur*. The last part, 'ant,' has the ahhhhhh sound, which usually is spelled with an 'a.' Sometimes also with 'au.' In this instance it is *ant*. A lot of you spelled that correctly. Bravo!"

"Yeah, I just knew it," Alex said.

"Well, and now you have a way to 'check it.' Let's try one more together, shall we? The next word is *absolutely*. Let me show you how it was spelled and then you can help fix the spelling, 'absoltlee.' Clap it and then ask yourself, 'Does this part have a short or long vowel sound?' Remember, each part needs at least one vowel. Caps off and try it!"

I reconvened the class and asked students to share their findings with their partners, as well as how they had thought about each part. Then I walked them through my thinking.

LINK

Send students off to edit their writing, using their editing checklists.

"Writers, don't forget to use your checklist as you look over your work today. You can try to spell your words a few different ways and you can think about each syllable in a word and ask, 'Does this part of the word have a short or long vowel sound?' You can also clap it out. You know other ways of spelling, as well. You can consult our word wall, think about word parts, and use other words you know to help you spell new words."

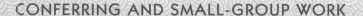

Supporting Students with Language and Conventions

THIS WILL BE YOUR LAST SESSION until the celebration. You will want to spend your time wisely as you confer and pull small groups. Your goal is twofold in this session. One, to help your students finish their writing and get their pieces ready for publication. Two, to support students with the development of their editing skills. Your students' checklists contain items about spelling, punctuation, and possibly even apostrophes. As you look at the end-of-the-year benchmarks for your students' language and conventions expectations, hold in mind what skills students need to master this year.

It will be helpful to identify long-term convention goals for individual students. Certainly, you can use your conference and small-group time to begin to address some of the new learning around conventions, whether this is punctuating sentences with clauses or using capital letters for more than just a title and the beginning of a sentence. Note which skills you want to carry with you into the next unit of study.

You may pull a small group of students who have not yet fully incorporated into their repertoire kindergarten and first-grade language conventions. World-class standards lay out a continuum of thinking about each of these areas from kindergarten through high school. You can pull a small group of students and conduct an interactive writing session to help students receive support and practice in any of these areas. Typically this might include students working on capitalization, adding ending punctuation to simple sentences, using commas in a list, and using beginning spelling patterns like CVC words.

Interactive writing can be a particularly supportive method and tool for working on spelling. If you find, through your spelling inventory and assessing students' daily work, that you have a small group of students who are working on spelling strategies and are emergent spellers or are working on what Donald Bear characterizes as the Letter-Name Stage (more similar to kindergarten or first grade), pull this group to first work in a shared text, and then to work on their own writing. Tailoring spelling strategies to your students is crucial. You may have a group of spellers who are working well above grade level. Pull those students together and work on thinking about the nuances of words.

MID-WORKSHOP TEACHING
Using the Word Wall to Fix Up Spelling

"Writers, remember how in first grade you all used the word wall *a lot* to spell words that you were learning? I want to remind you that you can still use the word wall to make sure you've spelled words correctly in your writing. The words up here on our wall are some of the most frequently used words in books. They also are really easy to misspell and overlook while you are editing. Also, there are words up there with certain endings highlighted, like *ed* and *er* and *ing*. Spend a little time, right now, looking at our word wall. Reread a few of the words on it and check to see if you used any of those in your writing. If so, double-check the spellings. Also check your endings to see if you've spelled *ed* or *ing* endings correctly. This is another tool to help you spell the best you can."

Fixing and Fancying Up Writing

Set students up to work in partnerships, fixing any remaining things in their writing for tomorrow's celebration.

"Writers, as you work on fixing your writing, remember that your partner can help you double-check some of the things on the editing checklist. Another pair of eyes can be helpful. Partner 1, can you share your piece with Partner 2? Partner 2, think about the checklist and use your editing eyes to help spot what Partner 1 *might* have missed. Partner 1, listen to Partner 2's suggestion. Sometimes another person can see things we missed. A partner is not always 'right,' but it is good to have a second opinion! Remember, you can always talk back if you disagree. You can have a spelling debate. Go ahead. Then I will give Partner 2 a chance to share with Partner 1."

A Celebration

ear Teachers,

Your children will now have spent six weeks learning the craft of narrative writing under the influence of some of the best children's book authors, and their work is a testimony to all they've learned. Next month, you and your children will embark on new terrain. This will be exciting, but it won't yield gorgeous texts like those you have before you now. So, this is a good time to invite the whole world in to see and to celebrate.

PREPARING FOR THE CELEBRATION

You'll certainly want to invite family members; chances are many of your children have written personal narratives about mothers and fathers, siblings and grandparents. You could also invite another class (last year's second-graders, who will appreciate seeing work that they've done themselves, or this year's first-graders, who will have something to look forward to), or you could invite colleagues or members of the community.

Whatever you decide, make a big deal of this day. This is the first celebration your students will experience as second-grade writers, and the work they have tackled thus far is no small feat. Not only have they studied texts closely, mining these for craft moves they have then unpacked and applied to their own writing, they have also made inquiries into their own writing identities and plans, thinking about how to make decisions that are purposeful and that reflect their intentions.

So live it up! You began this unit by introducing your children to some master writers; now, how about introducing your new class of master writers to their audience? You could take on the role of MC, welcome guests to your room, give them a brief synopsis of the work your students have done, and then spotlight just a few of your writers.

CELEBRATION

You might say something like, "Parents, grandparents, other caretakers, school leaders, and writers, we've gathered here to celebrate an extraordinary group of young writers. Please give a round of applause to Class 201, the world's new Master Writers." Then introduce just a few of your students in ways that they can replicate in a minute on their own in smaller groups: "Justin is famous in our class for being the first to try ellipses—and a lot of other things. He is enthusiastic about all things, bringing jazz-like energy to our classroom" (see Figure 19–1). Then read aloud a few lines from this first child's piece.

The Jazz Music

We were walking in the auditorium when I heard the jazz music. Everyone sat down and . . . the jazz music started.

Everyone started to dance . . . and before I knew it I was dancing too. The jazz music.

They played lots of songs and I went up on stage and I . . . was singing on stage with them. To the jazz music.

I hope there is going to be another performance soon.

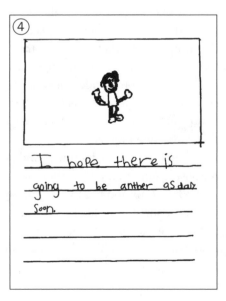

FIG. 19–1   Justin's writing shows that he made a conscious effort to use ellipses.

Introduce a second writer: "Lindsay is so good at making long stories out of small moments that she can write a whole book about the excitement of waiting for the elevator, carrying her friend, to arrive on her floor!" (see Figure 19–2).

> I waited and waited and finally the telephone that is for when someone was here to visit ring.
>
> Buzzzzzzzz. Mummy answered. She said, "Send them right up." I almost jumped out of my skin because that meant Annabel was here. Here!!! I ran to the door . . .
>
> I opened it and waited a little. Then I started to tell the elevator to hurry up. Then I heard talking and the sound of the elevator beeeppp. "Hello," I said. "Hello," said Annabel. And we both hugged each other.
>
> The waiting was over. I was happy. I knew it will be fun.

Then, you might send your children and their guests off to different corners of the room to introduce themselves in similar ways. Group children according to their writing circles. Explain to guests that they will play an active role in this next part of the celebration. Children will take turns introducing themselves and their work, perhaps naming one thing they have tried in their writing under the influence of a mentor

(text continues on p. 163)

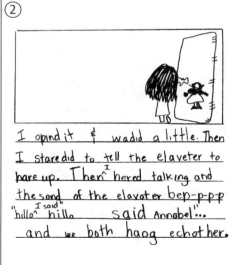
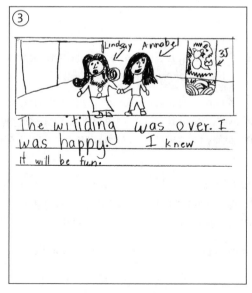

FIG. 19–2   Lindsay's writing that she shared for the celebration shows some of the craft moves she learned in this unit of study.

Awesome Christmas

"Jackson, when are we going to open presents?" I yelled. "Soon," said Jackson. So I went downstairs to play with Wii. I was playing Star Wars Force Unleashed. I was swinging the sword, shooting lightning, and choking good guys. When I got to the boss level, I was hitting the good guy. My mouth was wide open. My eyes popped open.

I could feel my win. "Yes, I'm going to win," I screamed. My mouth was wide open. I was jumping up and down. I finally beat the boss level. "Phew, that was a close one," I yelled. I was sweating. My face was red. I was fanning with my hand. Then I was going to get revenge on my evil master Darth Vader. But then . . .

My aunt called "time for presents." So I paused the game and shrieked, "I'm coming!" I dashed upstairs. I ran through the living room and to a chair. My heart was pumping so fast. "Phew, I almost missed presents time," I said calmly.

I was waiting for my cousins. I waited. I waited. I was thinking to myself, "Gosh, where are they," I yelled. So I checked everywhere then I went downstairs. I saw my cousin hiding and I pulled him out. My veins were popping. My face was red. "You guys are so not cool. You hid yourself. You're not cool." "Sorry," he said.

I pulled them upstairs. I dragged them across the floor. Then I threw them on the chair. My cousin got amazing gifts then it was my turn. My hands were shaking, butterflies were in my stomach. I opened my gift and . . . it was a DS. It was so cool so I played with it. "This is awesome," I screamed.

FIG. 19–3   Rehman's celebration piece illustrates his use of quotations.

author. Then, they will read aloud their piece, after which the guests and the other children in the writing circle will celebrate this work, pointing out craft moves they notice in the child's writing, and asking questions about what inspired the presenting writer to try out those moves.

Although you won't describe it this way, these mini-writing-circle celebrations will provide children a forum to practice their speaking, listening, and presentation skills, especially those outlined by world-class standards. They will be meeting in a diverse group of peers and adults, engaging in collaborative conversations, taking turns listening and talking, building on each other's talk, asking clarifying questions, presenting key ideas from a text read-aloud, and telling stories with descriptive details in audible voices.

AFTER THE CELEBRATION

After each child has had the chance to share and talk about his or her writing, gather the group together again, thank the visitors for coming, and let everyone say a quick good-bye. Then, tell your students that they are going to celebrate in one more way. "Writers, today you proved just how much you have learned over the past six weeks. You have worked hard and it shows. Guess what? Each of you is going to tell one more person how much you have learned. And that person is—a mentor author!"

Point to a stack of books that children have been studying this unit, and throw in some copies of the two texts you have studied together. Say, "Writers, when I came up with this idea, I had in mind that you would each write a letter to the author whose work you chose to study the past week. But you don't have to. You could instead write to Jane Yolen, or to Angela Johnson, or to another writer whose work you know well."

Before children write their letters, say a bit about what these might include. This is another opportunity for children to reflect on what makes for a powerful piece of writing. You might even have them turn and talk quickly about some things that might go into a letter of thanks to a mentor author. Certainly, they will want to say thank you, and chances are your children might also think to name what, exactly, they have learned from the author—the craft moves they have especially admired and tried out in their own writing. They might also include lines from the books they've studied that they especially loved. They might even include a copy of their published piece (you could make the copies to avoid children spending time rewriting their narratives).

You might also give children the option of researching on the computer whether their mentor authors have websites, like Jane Yolen does, on which fans can post messages. If so, they can opt to communicate in this way instead. However, there is nothing like an old-fashioned letter to make someone's day, and many authors send back letters to children who write to them.

Once your children have written their letters of thanks, give them a pocket of time to revise and edit these in the same ways that they have revised and edited their narratives. Remind them of the charts and tools around the room that they can draw on to be sure they have presented themselves and their work as intended. Soon children will be turning to information writing, a very different kind of writing that nonetheless draws on many of the same skills as narrative writing and letter writing. You will thus convey to your young writers that skills are transferable across different kinds of projects. Meanwhile, you will be setting them up to engage in the kind of work that Norman Webb outlines in his Depth of Knowledge as the highest level of cognitive processing (Level 4), i.e., synthesizing and applying knowledge across contexts. Most important, you will convey to your students that their writing matters—that it has an audience and place in the world—and that they will continue to grow as writers, experimenting with different texts, purposes, and craft as they set new goals for their writerly lives.

Best of luck,

Julia and Amanda